STOCKTON PAST

Views of central Stockton and Ropner Park.

STOCKTON PAST

Robert Woodhouse

Phillimore

1994

Published by
PHILLIMORE & CO. LTD.,
Shopwyke Manor Barn, Chichester, Sussex

ISBN 0 85033 906 5

Printed in and bound in Great Britain by
BIDDLES LTD.,
Guildford, Surrey

Contents

List of Illustrations

Acknowledgements

The author is indebted to the following people for their assistance in researching material and assembling the illustrations: Mrs. Joyce Chesney, Stockton Reference Librarian, Karen Leahy, Stockton Public Relations Department, Mark Rowland Jones, Stockton Museums Service, Dave Morrell for copying many of the original prints, Mrs. Ann Mason for allowing access to her private collection of postcards and his son, John Woodhouse, for preparation and typing of written material.

The following have kindly given their permission to reproduce illustrations: Cleveland County Council, Libraries and Leisure Department, 5, 44-46, 48, 56-58, 60, 63, 71, 83, 87, 89, 93, 94, 118, 122 and 125; Stockton on Tees Borough Council, 13, 20, 24-25, 39-40, 50, 53, 55, 77, 80-81, 90, 97, 101, 120-121, 126-127; Stockton on Tees Museum Service, 2, 4, 6-8, 14-15, 17, 23, 26-28, 32-34, 38, 41-43, 54, 59, 61-62, 64, 67-68, 72, 78-79, 85-86, 91, 95-96, 98-100, 102-104, 108-110, 112-117, 119 and 123. Mrs. Anne Mason, 3, 9, 16, 18-19, 21-22, 29-31, 35, 38, 49, 51-52, 66, 69-70, 76, 82, 84, 88, 92, 105-7 and 111; Dave Morrell, 1, 10-12, 124 and 128-39; North Tees NHS Trust, 73-75.

Introduction

A settlement has probably existed on the banks of the Tees at Stockton since the Anglo-Saxon period but the first documentary evidence appears in the Boldon Book of 1183, the Palatinate of Durham's equivalent of Domesday Book. The manor of Stockton was created soon after 1183 and in 1189 it was purchased by Bishop Pudsey, along with the royal manor of Sadberge.

During the medieval period the township was dominated by the bishops of Durham. Their manor house—or castle—at the southern end of the settlement was favoured by successive bishops and royal guests, but, although the port was mentioned in 1228 and a market charter was granted in 1310, Stockton was over-shadowed by Darlington, Hartlepool and Yarm.

With the ending of the palatinate's jurisdiction in the early 1500s, Stockton was able to extend trading activity outside the county, and by the late 17th century it was benefiting from Hartlepool's decline. Notable export activity included the shipping of lead and dairy produce to London, and in 1680 the Customs Office moved from Hartlepool to Stockton.

By the mid-18th century Stockton had taken on the appearance of a thriving Hanoverian township. With completion of the parish church, a new parish of Stockton was founded in 1713, and during 1735 a new Town House was built on the site of the tollbooth in the centre of the High Street.

Apart from river based industries such as ship building and sailcloth making, agriculture remained the main occupation for the Stockton area and the town became the centre of the south-east Durham agricultural region. Individuals from Stockton made headlines in several different walks of life during the 18th and early 19th centuries and future industrial expansion was heralded by the opening of the Stockton-Darlington Railway in 1825. Engineering and steelmaking became the town's main employers as the population increased rapidly during the 19th century.

This book aims to trace the development of Stockton from its early days under the bishops of Durham jurisdiction and through the period of prosperity in the 18th century to its changing fortunes in recent decades.

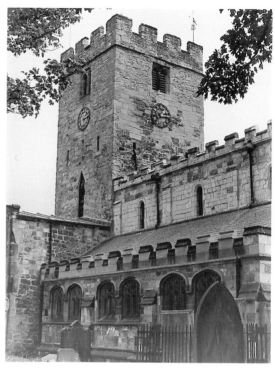

1 Granite boulder at Sadberge with inscription celebrating the Golden Jubilee of Queen Victoria—'Countess of Sadberge'.

2 St Mary's church, Norton, from the north side.

3 The interior of Norton parish church pre-1875.

Chapter One

Bishops of Durham

After the end of Roman rule in the north of England, a number of small settlements were established close to the northern bank of the Tees. The discovery of a large pagan burial mound at Norton (some two miles from Stockton) indicates the presence of a flourishing community in this locality between A.D. 450 and 650.

During the 10th century the Anglo-Saxon estate centred around Norton was given to the bishop of Durham by a son of the Earl of Northumberland as a mark of his high regard for St Cuthbert, patron saint of the bishopric. The parish of Norton covered approximately fifteen square miles along the north bank of the Tees, and Stockton was one of a number of small settlements within its boundaries. It remained part of the parish of Norton until the early 18th century.

Following William of Normandy's subjugation of the north of England, Walcher, a native of Lorraine, was installed as bishop of Durham in 1071. Four years later he was granted the earldom of Northumberland and this gave him both temporal and spiritual jurisidiction over the area between the rivers Tweed and Tees.

During the Middle Ages successive bishops ruled Durham as if they were kings. They exercised control over their own civil and criminal courts, had their own prison in Durham Castle, minted coins and established boroughs and markets by their own charters. Powers held by these mighty prelates included administration of forest law, the right to wreck and a court of admiralty—along with the right to levy customs dues at ports of entry such as Hartlepool.

The bishop's main hunting lodge was at Bishop Auckland and extensive estates within the county were centred on Darlington, Stockton, Easington, Chester le Street, Gateshead and Washington.

The first documentary reference to Stockton appears in the Boldon Book of 1183, the Palatinate of Durham's equivalent of Domesday Book. The name 'Stockton' indicates a 'tun' or 'village' belonging to the 'stoc' or 'monastery' of the bishop of Durham. This survey recorded that there were 11 villeins and six and a half farmers on the land at Stockton, and it also reveals that Stockton had a hall which was used by the bishop during his tour of the diocese.

The manor of Stockton was created shortly after 1183 and in 1189 it was purchased by Bishop Pudsey, along with the royal manor of Sadberge. Sadberge retained its importance as an administrative and judicial centre for several centuries. Under the bishop's commission, judges itinerant held a court of assize in the village until at least the middle of the 15th century and a County Court, presided over by the Sheriff of Sadberge, continued in use until the beginning of the 17th century. There was a jail for prisoners and nearby Gallows Hill is said to have served as a place of execution.

The earldom of Sadberge was one of the titles attached to the Crown of England and an inscription on a grey boulder at the centre of the village green states: 'This stone was placed here to commemorate the jubilee of Victoria, Queen of the United Kingdom, Empress of India and Countess of Sadberge, June 20 1887'. It was found 12ft. below the surface in making the reservoir. It had been detached from the rock in the west and deposited by a glacier.

No documentary evidence is available to indicate when Stockton gained a Charter of Incorporation but it is thought that the bishop of Durham made the town 'a borough by

4   Duck pond and village green at Norton.

prescription' in the middle of the 13th century. During this period Stockton, planned and planted by the bishop to compete with the neighbouring ports of Yarm and Hartlepool, was increasing in importance as a port and business centre and there was also considerable growth in population, for Bishop Thomas Hatfield's survey of 1384 mentions *tentes infra burgum* and *tentes extra burgum*—meaning those living within the borough and those outside.

Successive bishops of Durham paid regular visits to the manor house at Stockton. King John is said to have stayed there during 1214 in the company of Bishop Poicteu and alterations were carried out on the orders of Bishop Kellow in 1310. Further rebuilding work took place in

1376 and again under Bishop Langley (1406-37), who paid some eighty visits to the town during this period.

The 'special status' of Durham came to an end in 1536 when the Jurisidiction of Liberties Act considerably reduced the legal powers of the bishop of Durham.

During the late 16th century further restoration work was carried out on the bishop's residence at Stockton. In 1578 Bishop Barnes gave orders for building work to be carried out, and a fire during Bishop Matthew's period of convalescence in 1597 heralded the final demise of these extensive premises during the mid-17th century.

Chapter Two

Bishop's Castle or Manor House

Stockton Castle was built as a manor house owned by the bishops of Durham. Situated on land at the southern end of the High Street its boundaries extended along the river Tees and then ran through John Walker Square and Yarm Lane before turning left through Holy Trinity churchyard back to the banks of the Tees. The earliest written reference to a hall on this site is in the Boldon Book—a survey published by Bishop Puiset in 1183—but decorated stonework found during excavations in 1966 was dated to between 1150 and 1170 so there must have been a building here at an earlier date. The quality of the workmanship and decoration indicates that it was an impressive structure.

Successive bishops of Durham used the manor house as a location for entertaining guests

5 The last surviving building of Stockton Castle. This barn was converted into two castellated cowhouses in 1800 and was demolished on 29 June 1865. It stood on the corner of Bridge Road and Moat Street.

and as an occasional residence. King John stayed at Stockton in 1246, as a charter granted to the burgesses of Durham is dated there. Bishop Nicholas de Farnham retired from office in 1249 and spent most of the remaining eight years of his life at Stockton.

Alterations were carried out on the orders of Bishop Richard Kellow in 1310, but during the next few years Scottish raids caused widespread damage to this area and there was further building work in 1376. (At one time it became known as Stockton Castle.) There was another period of renovation under Bishop Langley (1406-37).

Account rolls for various years in the late 15th century provide information about buildings within the castle's boundaries. Extensive repairs were made to a 'great barn' during 1480-1 and there are also references to a common furnace and a bakehouse, which was roofed in 1503-4. A riverside staithe was built in 1515 at a cost of £7 17s. 11d. Documents from the years 1531-5 record ordination ceremonies at the chapel of the manor house during the month of September. Numbers of people involved in them indicate that it was a sizeable chapel and there was domestic accommodation for over forty people.

In 1543 Stockton Castle was garrisoned by Henry VIII's troops. This was in response to the failed rebellion by northern barons known as the Pilgrimage of Grace. An inquiry into the condition of the manor house of Stockton, commonly called Stockton Castle, leaves no doubt that the buildings were generally very 'decaied and ruynouse'. Some £1,600 was said to be needed to carry out repairs and, though documentary evidence is scarce, it seems that the chapel and domestic accommodation must

6 *(Left)* No. 9 Finkle Street. The property is said to be built with stone from Stockton Castle.

7 *(Above)* Buildings at the bottom of Castlegate (south side). The site was cleared in 1970 to make way for redevelopment.

have been made useable by 1586 when Bishop Barnes ordained eight deacons and eight priests in the building. Three years later Bishop Matthew fled to Stockton as plague spread through County Durham.

Civil War broke out in August 1640 and in the same month, following the defeat of Royalist forces at the hands of Scottish troops at Newburn, Bishop Morton fled to 'his castle at Stockton' before travelling south to York and London. The King's forces garrisoned Stockton Castle and it was considered important enough to be excluded from territories given up in the Treaty of Ripon (dated 1 October 1640).

After the Royalist defeat at Marston Moor, near York, in 1644, Stockton was taken by Scottish forces under the Earl of Callender and they remained there until 1647.

An order of parliament, dated 14 October 1645, sounded the death knell for Stockton Castle by ordering that this and several other garrisons in the north 'being placed there without the consent of both Houses of Parliament of England and their committees, may be speedily removed'.

A further order of parliament made on 26 February 1647 states 'that Stockton Castle be made untenable and the garrison dismantled'. Five months later, on 13 July, the House of Commons passed a resolution 'that the house doth concur with the Lords that the works about Stockton Castle made sithence these troubles be slighted and dismantled and the garrison dispersed'. In the same year a survey of the castle by Edward Colston and George Daile gave an impression of the state of the buildings and adjacent lands—'That the castle hath a great moate about it, but the same is now, for want of cleansing, filled up in part and within that moate hath heretofore been orchards and gardens, but all destroyed. There hath likewise been a parke, but the same hath been disparked'.

On 24 March 1648 the manor of Stockton was sold to William Underwood and James Nelthorpe for £6,165 10s. 2½d. and during the next four years the castle was rased to the ground.

One of the castle's buildings survived until the mid-1860s. Mentioned in one of the surveys of 1647 is 'The Barn' which 'hath been lately

8 The town's early insignia depicting a castle and anchor is a reminder of the Bishop of Durham's manor house (or castle) and the importance of shipping between the medieval period and the mid-20th century.

9 Engravings on this old postcard highlight buildings and structures that have featured prominently in Stockton's history. Stonework from the manor house was incorporated into the old *Blue Posts Hotel (top right)* and the wall adjacent to the gate *(bottom left)*.

built and is a very large one, built of stone and decays very little'. It was probably situated on the corner of Tower Street and Bridge Road but on 29 June 1865 the barn was sold and pulled down.

Amounts of stone from the castle were removed during the excavations of 1966 and are currently in use at Preston Hall Museum and the Green Dragon Heritage Centre in Theatre Yard. One item—'the Lion Stone'—was removed after demolition work in 1652 and turned up some years later in a farmyard at Elton. From there it was removed to the grounds of Colonel Sleigh's residence at Elton and in the 1920s it was rediscovered marking the burial place of a famous racehorse, 'Othello'. After spending some time on display in the vestibule of the old Borough Hall, it disappeared again (in the early 1930s) when the building was demolished. During 1952 it was rediscovered in a heap of rubble at the north end of the lake in Ropner Park and it now has a permanent place in the Green Dragon Heritage Centre. Until redevelopment schemes of 1970-1 got underway, traces of stonework from the castle

could be identified in the lower levels of buildings in Castlegate, Silver Street, Finkle Street and other streets between the High Street and the river.

Two cottages were built on part of the castle site soon after 1652 and were occupied for a time by Mr. H. G. Faber and Mr. Felix Cruse, but they were demolished shortly before the building of the Castle Theatre in 1907. The foundation stone of the Castle Building was laid by Mr. Richard Murray of Elm Park, Harrogate, on 3 October 1907 and Mr. William Kirk's company performed the opening play *The Lady of Lyons* at the theatre on 31 July 1908. After some sixty years of life the theatre closed down and the site was redeveloped during the early 1970s with a hotel complex. The area covered by the excavation of 1966 was within the Castle Brewery. Opened in 1856 by William Kilvington Kirk and John Kirk (to replace a small brewery of 1840), it was operational until the mid 1960s. The buildings were demolished as the site formed part of the redevelopment scheme for the east side of Stockton High Street.

Chapter Three

The Old Churches

St Mary's church at Norton was founded in the eighth century and during the medieval period it became the mother church for the population of Stockton. Worshippers from the developing township and adjacent villages faced a difficult journey during inclement weather, and in 1235 a chapel of ease was built on a site close to the parish church. Tradition suggests that it was dedicated to St Thomas à Becket—assassinated at Canterbury in December 1170—but there is no documentary evidence to support this.

By the late 17th century the chapel at Stockton had fallen into disrepair and Thomas Rud, curate of Stockton, organised plans to create a new parish for the town. The foundation stone of the parish church was laid on 5 June 1710 and two years later it was ready for use. A service of consecration took place on 21 August 1712 but it was some ten months later before Stockton became a separate parish from Norton. Galleries were added to the original building in 1719, 1748 and 1827 with the result that the interior became much darker. During the early 1890s major restoration work was carried out and this included removal of box pews and some galleries along with the repositioning of the pulpit on the north side of the church. Further alterations were made during the 20th century with the addition of a chancel (in 1906), Lady Chapel (during 1925) and

10 *(Above left)* In recent years Holy Trinity church was used by the Greek Orthodox church, but in late 1991 it was destroyed by fire. The east end is seen in this view.

11 *(Above right)* The north side of Holy Trinity church.

12 *(Right)* Interior of Holy Trinity church.

13 Contrasts in building styles with St John's church, Nolan House (tower block) and the gas works.

14 *(Left)* The frontage of Brunswick Methodist church in Dovecot Street. Opened in 1823 it has been converted for use as business premises.

15 *(Above)* Interior of Brunswick Methodist chapel in Dovecot Street.

church hall in 1976. A programme of restoration and redecoration was carried out during the early 1980s and a service of thanksgiving and rededication was held on 11 June 1984. In recent years the church's spacious interior—characterised by some superb bench ends—and fine acoustic qualities have made an ideal setting for choral and orchestral concerts.

Three years after victory at Waterloo ended the wars with France, the British government provided one million pounds to build churches

16 *(Above left)* The interior of St Mary's Roman Catholic church on Norton Road.

17 *(Above right)* Methodist chapel Sunday school at the rear of Brunswick Methodist chapel.

18 *(Below right)* St George's Presbyterian church on Yarm Lane.

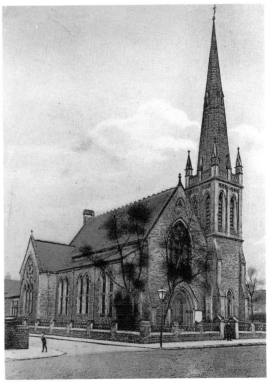

and Holy Trinity church may be one of these 'Waterloo churches'. Land for the building and large churchyard was provided by Bishop van Mildert, the last of the prince bishops of Durham, and this imposing Gothic-style church was consecrated on 22 December 1838. Its impressive west tower with flying buttresses and spire became unsafe and was demolished in 1957. During the post-war years shifting population trends brought smaller congregations and the church was closed. Members of the Greek Orthodox community used the premises during the 1980s, until a serious fire in October 1991 gutted the interior and left the building with an uncertain future.

Numbered among the places of worship which have already been demolished is the church of St John the Baptist. The parish of St John was set up in 1871 and the church was consecrated three years later. This distinctive red-brick building was constructed in the Basilican style and consisted of an apsidal chancel, nave with north and south aisles, and north porch. The site was cleared in 1980 and no trace of the church remains.

With the town's population shifting westwards during the late 19th century, the parish of St Peter was formed in 1875 and worshippers used a wooden building on land at the junction of Yarm Road and Cranbourne Terrace. After reconstructing the wooden church on the present site, plans were made for a permanent building

and the foundation stone was laid in 1880. The new church, Early English in style and constructed mainly with red bricks, was consecrated on 13 October 1881 by the Bishop of Durham, Bishop Lightfoot.

19   St Peter's church on Yarm Road. The Rev. Sale Pennington was the second vicar at the church.
20   St James' church, Portrack.

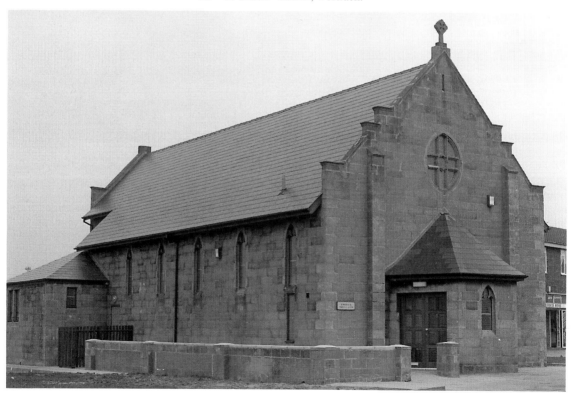

Movement of the population away from the town centre also resulted in closure of Nonconformist churches. Brunswick Methodist church in Dovecot Street has the date 1823 on a carved stone above the central doorway. The Sunday School premises in adjacent William Street were opened during the following year but both buildings are now used as business premises.

Paradise Row Methodist chapel in Church Road was opened in 1866 and forms an interesting contrast with the building in Dovecot Street. In addition to frontal twin towers it is also decorated with devils and skeleton dogs—unusual features for a Methodist place of worship. Church services ended in 1945 and the building is also currently in use as business premises.

Members of the Baptist community opened a small chapel in West Row in 1809 and, after enlarging the building in 1840, they moved to new premises in Wellington Street in 1869. A final move to the present red-brick building took place in 1902.

Several other 19th-century church buildings remain in use as places of worship and their prominent towers make them well-known local landmarks. These include St Mary's Roman Catholic church on Major Street, the work of Pugin whose designs were based on the Early English style. Initial stages were completed during 1841-2 with the tower being added in 1866 and south aisle, Lady Chapel, chancel, baptistry and sanctuary completed some four years later. Similarly impressive dimensions are displayed on the United Reform church of St Andrew and St George in Yarm Lane (built during 1875-6) and the Methodist chapel—dating from 1904—in nearby Yarm Road.

Chapter Four

The Town House

No record exists to indicate when the bishops of Durham granted borough status to the town of Stockton but reference is made to a farm or lease in later proceedings. The first such document—giving the burgesses of Stockton a number of basic rights and freedoms including the power to elect their own mayor and carry out their own local affairs—was probably granted by Bishop Hugh Pudsey in the late 12th century. Boundaries of the ancient borough of Stockton enclosed the land between the river Tees and West Row (in the west) and from Yarm Lane to Dovecot Street-Silver Street (in the north).

The first details about the town hall site appear in Hatfield's Survey of 1382 when reference is made to payment of fines, tolls and market fees at the mayor's house. By the early 17th century the building included accommodation for guests but in 1635 it is referred to by Phineas Pette, master shipwright to King Charles I, as 'a mean thatched cottage'. During the late 1600s the mayor's house was incorporated into a purpose-built tollbooth which

21 The Town House is shown surrounded by stalls on market day during the era of tram cars and horsedrawn vehicles.

22   Market day scene from the south-western side of the High Street.

23   Roadworks on the western side of the High Street during one of the many changes made
      to the surface and layout of the town's main highways.

24 Interior of the council chamber with commemorative plaques on either side of the castle and anchor insignia. The halberd, which was in use before the town was presented with a mace, is in the glass case between the windows *(centre right)*.

25 Harold Macmillan, former Prime Minister and M.P. for Stockton during the inter-war years, addressing Stockton town council in March 1968 after receiving the freedom of the town. The mayor, John Whitfield, was Stockton's last mayor before the establishment of Teesside County Borough.

was probably constructed with stone from the demolition of Stockton Castle. Survey work carried out in 1985 revealed dimensions of the tollbooth as 13 yards by seven yards, with external stone steps from which public proclamations could be made. The tollbooth included a small lock up for detaining local offenders, prisoners awaiting trial at Durham and convicted criminals awaiting deportation from the port of Stockton.

The town house was rebuilt on a square plan during 1735 and extended nine years later so that it included an inn and four bow-fronted shops. Building work in 1744 also included a second set of chimney stacks and clock tower with bell.

The first floor of the town house staged public functions and important ceremonies. These included a number of notable occasions in the first half of the 19th century. On 18 September 1810 a dinner was held in celebration of the opening of the cut in the river Tees between Stockton and Portrack, and initial plans were set in motion for the construction of a canal or railway from Stockton to the west Durham coalfield. Almost twelve years later, on 23 May 1822, the celebrations marked the laying of the first rail at St John's Crossing beside Bridge Road, and over a hundred guests attended the banquet that followed the arrival of Locomotion No.1 at Stockton on 27 September 1825. The whole town was in celebratory mood on 24 September 1827 for the visit of the Duke of Wellington and festivities concluded with a reception in the Assembly Room of the town house.

Engraved copper plates were installed on the Aldermanic Bench of the Council Chamber in Festival of Britain Year 1951. These highlight the achievements of two of Stockton's best known sons, Thomas Sheraton and John Walker. A third plate recalling the town's links with the Stockton-Darlington Railway was unveiled on 21 October 1983.

Between 1968 and 1974 the old borough of Stockton on Tees was part of the County Borough of Teesside but a reconstituted Stockton on Tees District became effective from 1 April 1974. The elected council of the borough meets in the council chamber— formerly known as the Assembly Room—at the town hall and a number of council committees are held in the nearby No.1 Committee Room. A highlight of recent years was the visit of H.M. Queen Elizabeth II and H.R.H. Philip, Duke of Edinburgh on 14 July 1977. During the day's official functions both the mace, presented by the Marquess of Londonderry in 1954, and the halberd, which was in use from 1820 to 1830, were on public duty together for the first time. This signified the link between the old and new boroughs of Stockton on Tees.

Chapter Five

The 17th and early 18th Centuries

During the 16th century Stockton suffered from the general economic and social decline that affected most of England. With a static or falling population, there was a run down in Stockton's industrial base and long standing institutions such as markets and fairs lapsed. At the beginning of the 17th century the situation changed considerably and by the late 1600s Stockton and Yarm had emerged as the most important trading centres between the rivers Tyne and Humber. Much of this prosperity was derived from trade with London (with butter shipments to the capital forming a major proportion of overall cargoes by the 1670s). Returning vessels brought goods such as rum, tobacco and tea and the cycle of growth was continued by an increased demand for ships. Shipyards and associated trades imported supplies of timber, flax, hemp and iron from northern European countries. A growing population in the capital brought an increased demand for domestic coal and expanding heavy industries added to the clamour for north east coal. Along with Whitby, Stockton supplied many of the coal-carrying vessels that plied the east coast route.

Both Yarm and Stockton prospered during this period and between roughly 1680 and 1750 there was extensive rebuilding work in each township. This period of regeneration is marked by the construction of several notable buildings. In 1680 the customs office moved from Hartlepool to Stockton and a new customs house was opened in 1730, the parish church opened in 1712 and the town house was completed in 1735. A new roadway was constructed along the riverside from Finkle Street to Castlegate during 1706 and between 1717 and 1720 streets

26 John Brewster was appointed curate at Stockton in 1776 and moved on to Redmarshall in 1805, Boldon in 1809 and Egglescliffe in 1814. He wrote some sixteen books on theology and his *History of Stockton-on-Tees* was first published in 1796. He died at Egglescliffe in 1842.

were cobbled. Streets were laid out on ground to the east side of the High Street between the parish church and the borough boundary. Silver Street and Bishop Street were developed during 1716 and Church Road by 1724. (The area on the west side of the High Street was not developed until 1823 when Brunswick, Albion, William, Skinner and Lodge Street were completed.)

A report dated 1760 describes the developing township:

27 No. 16 Finkle Street. Situated on the south side of the raised roadway, it was adjacent to the *Custom House Hotel*.

28 Mount Pleasant windmill was a landmark on the eastern side of Norton Road. Built shortly before 1785 it remained intact until about 1920.

Stockton is finely situated and most beautifully laid out, the principal street is about fifty yards broad, with a town house and shambles in the middle of it, and it is a quarter of a mile long. Two streets are parallel with it from the east for about two hundred yards, and there are three or four streets which lead from it to the quays and bank, for there is a quay at each end; and to the east they build ships. Beyond the church (handsome and well built) is a bowling green with buildings on three sides of it, among which is a store house for giving out of flax to spin, as they have a great manufacture of sail cloth, and other coarse cloths. They have also an export of corn, butter, bacon and lead.

Chapter Six

Crossing the River

Throughout the medieval period Yarm bridge was the lowest crossing point on the Tees and until the late 18th century the township of Stockton relied on ferries (and fording points) for passengers and cargoes. The first mention of a ferry is in the Boldon Book of 1183 which states that 'the passage of the water pays 20d.' and it also refers to land on the Yorkshire side of the river which would be leased as a landing place for the ferry. Entries in the Great Rolls show that by 1306 the rent had risen from 20d. to 2s. 6d.

Bishops of Durham leased out all properties and services under their jurisdiction and Bishop

Hatfield's survey of 1380 shows 'the passage of the water with the little boat' was leased for 53s. 4d. During this early period few names of leaseholders are known but from the mid-16th century onwards arrangements are well documented. The lease payment included not only the ferry but also 'the shops under the Tollbooth', 'the common bakehouse' and 'the new close in the West Row'.

In March 1762 an Act of Parliament was obtained 'for building a bridge across the River Tees at or near the ferry at Stockton'. The foundation stone was laid in 1764 and the last of five arches was completed in 1768. Built

29 Victoria Bridge—opened 20 June 1887.

20

30 View of the Tees and riverside industries from Victoria Bridge. The postcard is dated 1905.

31 Victoria Bridge (completed in 1887) and *Bridge Hotel* at Thornaby. The postcard is dated 1906.

32 Victoria Bridge and piers of the earlier bridge in the foreground.

33 Stockton riverside in the 1930s. Tall buildings on the High Street and the tower of the parish church are seen in the background.

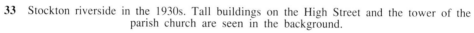

34   View of the river with Craig Taylor's shipyard on the southern bank.

35   Corporation Wharf with the *Manoela Victorino* at its mooring. Finkle Street is seen beyond the ship with *Custom House Hotel (left)* and the premises of Raimes and Co. *(right)*.

36 Riverside at the rear of Black Lion Yard.

entirely of stone, the bridge measured 72 ft. in length and 21 ft. wide including three feet of walkway for pedestrians. The bridge was in use by 1769 but the official opening did not take place until 1771. Tolls were charged for crossing the bridge so that the bishop of Durham's rents (totalling £93 per year) and the cost of building the bridge (which amounted to about £8,000) could be repaid. Toll charges ranged from ½d. for pedestrians to 8d. for horse-drawn carriages.

The bridge attracted a great deal of traffic and income from tolls was far beyond estimates—with the result that the debt was cleared by 1813. As Stockton prospered with the new crossing point so Yarm's river traffic declined and there were accusations that the arches had been made particularly low in order to restrict the movement of vessels upstream. As local hostility towards the tolls continued a riot occurred on 24 September 1819. Gates at the bridge were hauled down and thrown into the river before order was restored. Trustees soon agreed to pay off the accrued sum of £2,643 to the bishop and in 1821 the bridge was declared free of tolls.

The amount of traffic using the bridge continued to increase and in 1858 it was widened and given an improved surface but before long there were calls for a new bridge. In 1876 it was proposed that a new bridge should be built but it was another four years before the idea was officially adopted. An Act of Parliament in 1881 allowed work to get underway and the cost of the completed structure—£85,500—was over double the original estimate. It measured 300 ft. in length, with a centre span of 110 ft. and overall width of 60 ft. (which was more than three times as wide as the old bridge). A formal opening ceremony was held on 20 June 1887; with Her Majesty's permission, the bridge was named after Queen Victoria in her golden jubilee year. Victoria bridge became a vital link on one of the main approaches to Stockton town centre and in June 1988 its prominence was highlighted by the installation of floodlighting on each pillar.

Many of Stockton's menfolk were employed in foundries or shipyards on the Yorkshire bank of the river and used a private crossing service, Kelly's Ferry, to make the short river crossing

37 Ferry boats transferred workmen from Stockton to foundries and other heavy engineering premises on the Thornaby bank. Best known of these businesses was Kelly's Ferry.

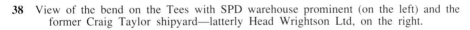

38 View of the bend on the Tees with SPD warehouse prominent (on the left) and the former Craig Taylor shipyard—latterly Head Wrightson Ltd, on the right.

to and from their workplace. The ferry ran from Sugar House Green and Cleveland Row on the Stockton bank across to the end of Trafalgar Street in Thornaby and the fare is said never to have increased to more than ½d. per passenger.

In 1830 the Stockton and Darlington Railway was extended from the terminus on the river bank at Stockton into Middlesbrough (or Port Darlington as it was known). A suspension bridge, designed by the leading engineer in this type of construction—Samuel Brown—carried the track across the Tees. It measured 412 ft. in length, with a main span of 281 ft. and the deck which measured 16ft. in width was suspended from 12 chains at a height of 20ft above the river level. Such a structure proved to be quite incapable of carrying locomotives without unacceptable movement and it was soon replaced by a multi-span girder bridge. The later replacement, dating from 1907, marks the site of these earlier crossing points.

Completion of the Stockton-Thornaby diversion (A66 Penrith-Middlesbrough trunk road) in May 1981 provided another crossing point in the form of the Surtees Bridge just a few yards upstream from the railway bridge.

On the opposite river bank from Stockton town centre a £500 million development—known as the Teesdale site—is underway and on 23 September 1992 Princess Diana officially opened the road bridge that links the new development with central Stockton. Built at a cost of £3.5 million, it incorporates 3,000 cubic metres of concrete, 160 miles of reinforcement and 360 tons of structural steelwork. Blue pearl granite-clad pillars at each corner of the superstructure add an imposing air to the bridge. It was named after Princess Diana and represents the ninth river crossing in the borough of Stockton.

Chapter Seven

Places of Entertainment

Provincial theatre enjoyed a period of prosperity during the 18th century but the country's only purpose-built theatres were to be found in London. Playhouses were usually adapted to a standard size—measuring about sixty feet by thirty, and about thirty feet to roof pitch—and were pit and gallery theatres, with boxes added at a later date. Richmond (in North Yorkshire) has a fine fully-restored theatre of this type and

the building in Theatre Yard at Stockton is of similar design. It began life as a tithe barn but was converted to a theatre in 1766 by Thomas Bates, manager of a company of comedians.

For some twenty years the theatre prospered as one of a number of venues in North Yorkshire and South Durham that were visited by Bates' touring company but during 1786 ownership passed to James Cawdell, a well known actor

39 *(Above left)* Georgian Theatre and Green Dragon Gallery in Theatre Yard.

40 *(Above right)* Gable of Georgian theatre building *(left)* close to restored warehouse in Green Dragon Yard. The warehouse dates from between 1790 and 1810 and detailed records of 1813 show that the ground floor was used for stabling horses and floors above partly used as a Calvinist meeting house. During the Victorian period it was raised in height from three floors to four and was converted into a warehouse. It continued in use as a warehouse until 1979 when it was purchased by Stockton Council. Recent conversion work uncovered a circular brick-lined drinking well in Green Dragon Yard and a water cistern measuring seven feet square and five feet deep.

from the period. He inherited considerable debts from Thomas Bates but soon showed himself to be a successful businessman and made sizeable profits from his theatrical interests. In 1798 he rented the Stockton theatre to Stephen Kemble, a member of the famous theatrical family but neither Kemble nor a succession of other owners made it pay as well as Cawdell.

Stephen Kemble made his farewell appearance, as Falstaff, on 6 July 1815. He had made improvements to the building and in 1818 there were further alterations when Anderson and Faulkner installed boxes. There are few details about the succession of owners during the next 40 years but it is known that one of the last companies to appear at the theatre (in 1861) was Mr. Powell's Leicester Players. During the 1850s it was known as the 'Royal' but by this time music halls were becoming the most popular form of entertainment in the north of England and the theatre was soon to degenerate into the 'Oxford Music Hall'. The building was later converted for use as a Salvation Army head-quarters and then became a sweet factory. During the 1970s Stockton council carried out restoration work on the premises and in recent years it has again staged musical concerts and theatrical occasions.

The New Theatre Royal (replacing the Georgian theatre) was opened on a site adjacent to Yarm Lane on 6 August 1866. In 1885 there

was a serious fire scare and the building narrowly escaped destruction. The new fire station in West Row was not yet completed and fire-fighters were summoned by the sounding of a bell in the Town Hall's cupola. A fire drill was held on 12 September 1887 and the audience of 1,404 people filed out of the building in two minutes.

During 1905 one week's performances included *Hamlet* on Wednesday, *Richard III* on Thursday and Saturday, and *New Men and Old Acres* on Friday—at a cost of 12s. for three performances. On 28 August 1906 the theatre was burned to the ground and it was then taken over by a former mayor of Stockton, Alfred Lewis, and his brother, Charles. For a few years the building was used as a rollerskating rink and during the First World War the Local Volunteer Reserve was based in the premises.

In the 1920s the Lewis brothers opened the building as the Maison de Danse and it became the most popular social venue in Stockton. An oval shaped dance floor of Canadian maple was installed for generations of dancers to enjoy music by Jack Marwood's band. They appeared at this venue—affectionately known to local people as 'the jazz'—for over forty years but musical fashions changed and the building closed in 1964. It was demolished soon afterwards.

The Royal Star Theatre in Bishop Street was opened in 1878 at a cost of £8,000. An impressive frontage was matched by gold-leaf

41 *(Above left)* Workers at J.F. Smith and Co.'s Nebo Confectionery works. The building was used as a theatre from 1766 until the 1860s.

42 *(Right)* Theatre Royal on Yarm Lane, photographed in 1922.

decor on the ceiling (added at a cost of £220 in the early months of 1883) but soon afterwards, on 3 April 1883, the building was destroyed by fire. It was rebuilt and opened as a music hall— The Grand Theatre of Varieties—in 1891 but just eight months later, on 12 April 1892, the premises were again ravaged by fire. Again it was reopened as a theatre and local press reports give interesting details of shows in the late 1890s—

21 December 1897, Grand Theatre Stockton: There was a crowded house at this place of amusement yesterday, when an excellent combination of first class artistes were accorded a hearty reception, the whole performance being given in such a manner as to guarantee the Grand a successful week. The artistes included the Ross Combination in 'Mr Maloney's troubles' assisted by the marvellous midgets; Miss Mabel Cowley serio-comic and low comedy artiste; Allan McAshell conjuror and funny patterer; Sister Powers' skirt, step and skipping rope dancers; Ashley and Beach negro comedians; Will Saunders, comedian and leg mania artiste; Queeni Palmer serio and ballad vocalist; Dueman, conjuror and electrician; Harry Dashwood, character comedian and actor vocalist; and James Curran, London, star comedian and parody King.

6 June 1899, The Grand, Stockton: An excellent programme is being submitted at the Grand Theatre this week. Amongst the nine members are three or four real good turns and the audience was not slow to recognise this last evening. Mdlle Irma Orbosany introduces 25 cockatoos which are exceedingly well trained and go through some clever feats. Messrs Chivers and Je Monti are well termed 'the skatorial wonders' whilst another good turn is that of Felix de Maree with his performing pony and horse back riding baboon 'Tess'. The two animals have undergone a complete tuition and the entertainment given by them is well worth a visit alone. Mr Arthur Bright, Mrs Ella Beresford, Miss Marie Mason and Mr Josh Higgins render vocal items of a 'catchy' character and Messrs Raleigh and Raleigh will take a lot of beating in the contortionist business ....

During the period 1932-6 the Grand was the only live theatre venue in Stockton but it closed in 1936. Reopened as the Plaza Cinema, it continued in use until 1959. For several years it was used to store furniture and when fire broke

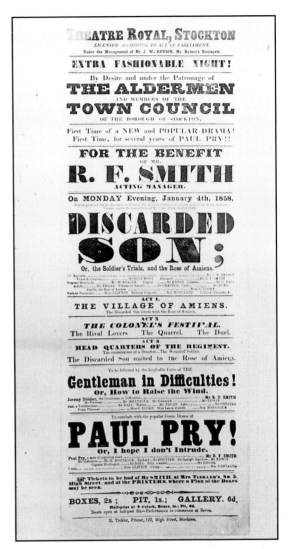

43 Play bill from the Theatre Royal advertising the programme for 4 January 1858.

out on 28 June 1962 some 300 seats were destroyed—but the building survived. The premises were finally demolished in 1960 to make way for the Quayside Relief Road.

The Hippodrome on the corner of Dovecot Street and Prince Regent Street was opened in 1905 and owned by North Eastern Entertainments (the Metcalfe family) from 1914 to 1958. On 21 March 1915 a concert was held at the theatre in aid of the Hartlepool Bombardment Fund (following the attack on Hartlepool in December 1914) and it became a touring theatre for pre-West End shows between the wars. A well known figure was commissionaire, 'Tippler Nolan', who boxed Jack Johnson in an exhibition bout at the theatre. Fire wrecked the building on 8 November 1932 and when it reopened it operated as a 'talkie' theatre until 1946 when variety shows returned. Numbered among star names who appeared during this period are Richard Briers, Charlie Chester, Julia and Margaret Lockwood, Des O'Connor and Anna Neagle.

Many local people have fond memories of amateur theatrical productions at the Theatre during the immediate post-war period. These came to an end on 17 March 1973 with the final performance of the Stockton Stage Society's production of *My Fair Lady*. The theatre was then converted into Teesside's first multiple cinema with three small screens and renamed 'the Classic'. It was then sold to the Cannon chain but, faced with competition from the Show-case cinemas at Teesside Park and a major town centre redevelopment scheme, the cinema closed for the last time on 2 September 1993.

The Globe cinema building on the High Street is the third to stand on this site this century. The first theatre was built before the First World War but was demolished during 1925-6 and replaced by premises with seating for 1,200 patrons. This building closed for rebuilding work on 20 April 1935 and 16 December 1935 the third 'Globe' reopened (an unusual feature of the structure is the amount of seating below ground level—with the balcony only 20ft. above the pavement).

'Live' theatre ended at the Globe during 1936 and in the following year it reopened as a super cinema on the ABC Circuit. Occasional live productions included opera, ballet and an annual Christmas pantomime. During the 1960s a number of well known pop groups attracted huge numbers of adoring fans. The Lipthorpe brothers, who owned the well-known Club Fiesta, made an attempt to revive the Globe's status as a theatre venue but this venture was short lived. Furnishings were sold and the building was opened in 1978 as a Mecca Bingo hall.

The Regal was opened on a High Street site on 22 April 1935. It always operated as a picture house and was later re-named The Odeon. The original building was demolished in 1966 and a new Odeon opened two years later. This cinema closed in 1982 and the site was re-developed as a night club, The Mall.

Exchange Hall occupied a site on the west side of the High Street. First opened

Globe Theatre, Stockton-on-Tees.

44   The Globe Theatre at the northern end of the High Street.

45 View of the west side of the High Street on market day showing 'the Cinema' in a central position.

46 The Hippodrome on the corner of Prince Street and Dovecot Street opened in 1905. In recent years it was renamed the Classic—then the Essoldo, and finally the Cannon, before closure on 2 September 1993.

in 1875, it was converted to show motion pictures in 1910 and the name was later changed to The Cinema. The building was damaged by fire on 28 February 1937 but re-opened on 13 June 1938. It closed as a picture house during 1964 and now stages Essoldo Bingo sessions.

Other small scale town centre places of entertainment include the News Theatre and Turner's Theatre.

(Information on the open-air theatre in Ropner Park is included in the chapter entitled Open Spaces.)

The Entertainers

Stockton has produced a number of notable names in the world of entertainment. Heading this list are three people with very different creative talents.

William Thomson Hay was born at 23 Durham Street on 6 December 1888. His family soon left Stockton and moved to Lowestoft where he showed up well at school. His family moved north again before he could take examinations but after leaving school began a career which was to make him Will Hay, one of the most successful British Music Hall stars to enter films. He was noted for school-room sketches playing a tyrannical yet hopeless schoolmaster and some of his films became classics of the British cinema—*Oh, Mr Porter*, *Windbag the Sailor*, *The Black Sheep of Whitehall*, *Convict 99* and *The Ghost of St Michael's*. His screen association with Graham Moffatt and Moore Marriott became, perhaps, the most famous in British film history. Before and after the First World War he became a favourite with the Royal Family and entertained them at Royal Variety Shows and private functions.

Off screen he lived a solitary life and involved himself in scientific subjects, most notably astronomy, and he is credited with discovering the white spot on the planet Saturn. Another of Will Hay's interests was flying and he became one of the first British civil pilots. Following the breakup of his marriage, there was no love interest in his films though in private life he was often accompanied by attractive women. Will Hay died on Easter Monday 1949.

Ivy Close was born at Stockton in 1890 and achieved instant fame in 1908 when she won the *Daily Mirror* beauty contest. Her dreamy sylph-like brand of loveliness was painted by Arthur Hacke of the Royal Academy and she appeared in a week-long show at the town's Castle Theatre soon after winning the beauty title, but then began to make films. Early appearances for the British film magnate, Cecil Hepworth, included *Sleeping Beauty* and *Dream Paintings* and, during 1914, Ivy Close made her first feature length film *The Lure of London*. In 1916 she began to make comedies for the famous Kalem Company in Florida with many of her films directed by her husband Elwin Neame. He was tragically killed in a car accident in 1923 but Ivy Close's career continued with character parts in French and German films such as *La Rue* (1920) and *Der Fidele Bauer* (1927). She appeared in a total of 44 films between 1912 and 1929 but as her youthful beauty faded she was forced to accept crowd parts and theatrical tours.

Her son, Ronald Neame, continued the family's connection with the film industry as a director and said of his mother, 'in her time ... she was one of the top five British stars'. Ivy Close died at Goring, Sussex, on 4 December 1968.

47 Doreen Stephens, Stockton-born singer.

Stockton produced a number of notable personalities in the music world but pre-eminent among these was Doreen Stephens. Born in the town on 7 November 1922, she was educated at Richard Hind Central School and first worked in a local music shop. She started singing at concerts and dances at the age of nine, and five years later she was 'spotted' by another local-born star of the entertainment world, Jimmy James. Jack Hylton included her in his road show 'Secrets of the BBC' and soon promoted her to his own big stage band. She went on to appear with the band at the London Palladium at the age of fifteen. This talented young singer went on tour with a stage version of radio's *Band Wagon*, starring Arthur Askey, and when war broke out in 1939 she rejoined Jack Hylton's band for a trip to France. During this tour she entertained troops in a show which included Gracie Fields and Maurice Chevalier. In 1940 she joined Maurice Winnick's band for performances in Palestine, Italy and the Middle East.

The post-war years saw her spend two years with the Squadronaires (1946-8) before embarking on a solo career which included an appearance at Middlesbrough Empire Theatre in 1949. From 1950 she spent 12 years with Billy Cotton and in two of her three Royal Command Performances with the band she was accompanied at the piano by her cousin—another Teessider—Bert Waller. During the early 1960s she suffered increasing ill-health and died in 1965 at the age of forty-two.

Chapter Eight

Local Government

The municipal development of Stockton dates back to the 13th century. Although the town is designated a corporate borough by prescription, it is believed that its charter of incorporation was signed by King John during a visit to Stockton Castle sometime between 1201 and 1208. Recorded evidence is scarce and the first mayor is Robert Burdon who held the office in 1495.

Increasing wealth and commercial development during the 18th century led to a growth of civic pride and in 1718 an order was made for the whole of the borough to be paved and for the setting up of wells and pumps. Until 1852 the settlement of Stockton was divided into two parts. One known as 'the borough' contained 17 acres and was governed by the corporation with freehold ownership for citizens. The other sector, 'the town', where land was held copyhold or leasehold (under the vicar and the vestrymen), was outside the jurisdiction of the corporation. Plaques were set in pavements on the High Street to mark the boundary line between the 'town' and 'borough'. In 1852 the Stockton Extension and Improvement Act extended the municipal borough from 17 to 1,189 acres and arranged for better provision of drainage, paving and lighting of the roadways.

Another Extension Act of 1869 further extended the boundaries of the borough and greatly increased the powers of the corporation in relation to highways, streets and public health. It also allowed the levying of a general rate to

48 Section of Stockton-on-Tees mace showing the pestle and mortar of John Walker, inventor of the friction match.

help meet the costs of implementing the Act. Under another Act of 1889 the borough was increased in size to include the township of Hartburn and the parish of Norton, giving the borough a total of 5,561 acres.

Post-war building schemes revealed the need to extend boundaries yet again and on 1 December 1951 an order of Parliament confirmed proposals to include land in the parishes of Norton and Elton—extending the borough to 6,084 acres.

Chapter Nine

Open Spaces

The town's first park was the gift of Sir Robert Ropner. Extending over 39½ acres of land—known as Hartburn Fields—on the western edge of the township, it was officially opened by the Duke and Duchess of York (later to become King George V and Queen Mary) on 4 October 1893.

A local newspaper reported that it had 'been tastefully laid out and artistically finished and planted with shrubs and forest plants. In laying out the park, the object kept in view has been to secure a series of graceful curves forming walks and avenues with raised mounds at intervals ornamentally shaped and planted to shield the grounds from inclement weather and cold winds'.

The 'Golden Gates' on Hartburn Lane gave access to a wide tree-lined avenue with an ornamental fountain at its head. On a nearby site, the Dodshon memorial drinking fountain was re-erected in the middle of a rockery (it had stood on the High Street since 1878). A cricket ground, bowling green, quoits green and tennis courts provided recreational opportunities

49   Ropner Park photographed from the air. Oxbridge Lane runs diagonally *(top right)* and Hartburn Lane is seen in the bottom left-hand corner.

and band concerts on Thursday evenings and Sunday afternoons continued for many years. Ropner Park became one of the town's most popular meeting places and in 1951 an open air theatre was built for performances of light operas and plays. The basic layout of the park remains unchanged but the bandstand and open-air theatre have been demolished and the 'Golden Gates' have been replaced by less ornamental ironwork. In 1932 land was bought adjacent to the Newham Grange Housing Estate and it was laid out with flower beds enclosing bowls and tennis courts, playing fields and a playground for small children.

Preston Hall and its surrounding parkland overlooking the Tees was the home of the Eden

50   (*Left*) Ornamental fountain in Ropner Park.

51   (*Top right*) Ropner Park lake.

52   (*Below*) Ropner Park lake and walkways.

53 Ropner Park bandstand.

54 Open-air theatre—built in 1951 to celebrate the Festival of Britain—in Ropner Park.

55 Preston Hall viewed from the north.

family until 1820, when it was sold to David Burton Fowler of Yarm. He built the hall in 1825 and less than a year later a section of the Stockton-Darlington railway line was completed close to the northern boundary of the park. On his death in 1825 the estate passed to his great nephew, Marshall Robinson, who assumed the family name and it continued in the Fowler family until 1882 when a Prussian, Emil Hugo Oscar Robert Ropner, purchased the estate.

The Ropner family made an important contribution to Stockton's development in the late 19th century. Their ship building business provided employment for local folk and Colonel Ropner, as he was then known, presented a public park to the townspeople in 1890. As Sir Robert Ropner, he made alterations to the family home at Preston Hall. The addition of a heavy stone porch and conservatory transferred the frontage from the side overlooking the river to the section facing on to the Stockton—Yarm Road. Leonard, the youngest of Sir Robert's five sons, inherited Preston Hall in 1924 and on his death in 1937 the premises were taken over by Ashmore, Benson and Pease.

Plans to develop the parkland with housing and amenities were turned down in 1944 and in July 1947 Stockton Corporation took over the estate and hall for development as a public park and museum. The museum was opened on 3 June 1953 by Alderman C. W. Allinson and

an important feature of the museum's displays was the collection of arms, armour, powder flasks, pewter and snuff boxes which had been left to the Borough of Stockton by Colonel G.O. Spence. Alterations during the winter months of 1968-9 saw the construction of galleries illustrating social life from about 1750-1900. It was re-opened as the Preston Hall Museum of Social History in April 1969.

In the early 1970s two outstanding works of art were re-discovered on the upper floor of the hall (they had formed part of the Clephan Bequest). Experts identified them as *Mustering of the Warrior Angels* completed in 1833 by Joseph Mallord William Turner and *The Dice Players* by the French artist, Georges de la Tour (1593-1652).

Recent developments have seen the creation of a north country street of the 1890s. Shops on Walker Street include a drapery, pawnbroker's, ironmonger's, police station and bookshops while other premises are occupied by working craftsmen such as a farrier, blacksmith and woodworkers.

Sectors of the parkland have been re-styled with animal enclosures, children's play areas and nature walks. In May 1987 a £140,000-aviary was opened and the emphasis on the natural world continued with the opening of Europe's largest butterfly farm, Butterfly World, in 1991.

Chapter Ten

Inns and Taverns

Many of the town's taverns were an integral part of the community. Along with the local church, they were a focal point for the population. Some had interesting architectural features, often the name of the pub sign had particular interest, and many gained an amount of folklore (including a ghostly presence).

Stockton's oldest inn was the *Blue Posts Hotel*. The building was situated on the west side of the High Street and gained its name from a pair of Frosterley marble pillars (said to be from Stockton Castle) which were built into

the structure by Rowland Burdon in the late 18th century. In recent times the premises were renamed *Trader Jack's*.

The town's next oldest inn was the *Custom House Hotel* at the bottom of Finkle Street. It was built in the late 17th century as a private residence but was licensed by 1717 when it is mentioned in the will of Mrs. Emma Redman (she had bought the property from Mr. Robert Spearman sometime before). Many of the town's inns incorporated a small kiln where beer was brewed for sale and this practice continued into

56 The *Spread Eagle Hotel* on the north side of Dovecot Street.

57 The *Green Bushes* in Yarm Lane. This neo-Georgian-style building replaced earlier premises of the same name in the late 1890s.

the 19th century. The *Custom House Hotel* brewed its own beer until 1879 when the premises were sold to Stockton on Tees Corporation. The local brewing company, J. W. Cameron Ltd., acquired the property on 30 June 1896 and it continued to trade until the late 1940s. It stood empty for a number of years before being demolished as part of the riverside redevelopment scheme.

Several other public houses stood close to the riverside. These included the *Baltic Tavern* (no.18 Quayside) which was previously known as the *Blue Anchor Tavern*, and continued to trade until the late 1960s. Nearby was the *Ship Launch Inn* (no.27 Quayside) and the *Greyhound Inn* which closed in the mid 1960s. Features of this building included the concert room upstairs and the Captain's Bar where ships' crews had been paid at the end of a voyage.

Closer to the centre of town, the *Star Inn*, on Garbutt Street, closed on 11 April 1963 and the *Grand* stopped trading in 1969. The century-old *King's Head* traded into the early 1970s. The *Regent Hotel* on Nelson Terrace was demolished to make way for extensions to Littlewoods Ltd. It contained 12 bedrooms and was a stop over for celebrities such as Charlie Chaplin and Julie Andrews when they appeared at the nearby Hippodrome.

Another public house with theatrical connections is *The Theatre* in Yarm Lane. Built by Thomas Wright, a soda manufacturer, it opened for business on 8 July 1870 and the first landlord was John Moody. Its name and decor are linked with the former Theatre Royal which stood nearby and the premises continue to trade today. Another town centre tavern where the accent is on tradition is the 200-year-old *Sun Inn* on Knowles Street. It occupies a corner section of the old churchyard adjacent to the parish church and, during recent building work, human remains were unexpectedly unearthed below the building.

In the early 1870s there were said to be as many as 108 licensed houses in the town and, although many of these had closed by the late 1920s, it was still possible to stand on Grey Horse Corner—at the junction of Yarm Lane and the High Street—and count a dozen hotels in close proximity. The *Grey Horse Inn* was itself a landmark but on the east side of the High Street there were several fine coaching inns. The *Vane Arms* was a stopping place for coaches linking east coast towns. In 1798 it is

58 The *King's Head* in Garbutt Street.

59 The *Vane Arms* and *Black Lion* hotels on the east side of the High Street. These buildings were cleared for redevelopment during the summer of 1970.

said to have had stables with standings for 26 horses, loose stabling for 30, two granaries and a blacksmith's forge. Adjacent to the *Vane Arms* was the *Black Lion Inn* which gained an outstanding reputation for service, and along the same stretch of the High Street stood the *William IV*. All these fine frontages were demolished in the late 1960s to make way for the Castle Centre development.

Another well known local landmark, the *Queen's Hotel*, met a dramatic end in January 1981 when it was badly damaged by fire and had to be demolished.

Many of the licences from town centre premises were transferred to hotels on the newly developed estates. The *Rimswell Hotel* on Bishopton Road received the licence from the *Custom House Hotel* in 1948. It was the town's first new post-war hotel and was built on land purchased from I.C.I. Ltd. (the name was derived from the Victorian mansion which stood on nearby land and was demolished to make way for the housing estate). The hotel's official opening took place on 29 July 1955. *The Maple Hotel* on Dover Road at Ragworth took over the licence from the *Star Inn*, Garbutt Street (closed on 11 April 1963) and, as amenities were provided on estates that were developed in the 1960s and 1970s, the *Mitre* was opened on Harrowgate Lane—close to the Bishopsgarth and Rimswell estates—on 10 January 1962.

Chapter Eleven

A Place for Learning

Stockton has a strong claim to have been the location for the country's first Sunday school. Edmund Harvey, born in the town in 1698, had a workshop in Finkle Street, and it was here that he set up a form of 'ragged school' where six poor boys were given a basic education. Pupils were also clothed and fed on the premises and part of the daily routine included attendance at morning service (at the nearby parish church). On Sundays they were taught about the scriptures. In the late 1760s places were made available for six poor girls and they received tuition in needlework from a female teacher.

Edmund Harvey, a pewterer by trade, was far-sighted in other respects and proposed alterations in the course of the river Tees. His plans were not followed up at the time but during the early 19th century these schemes were revived and carried out. He died in 1781 aged eighty-three.

In 1721 a charity school was opened in premises close to the parish church. Twenty boys paid voluntary subscriptions and wore 'habits blue and faced with yellow'. They were given a bible and common prayer book and tuition consisted of 'writing, reading, arithmetic and the principles of religion'. Girls were admitted in 1759 and were taught 'sewing, spinning and the honest skills' in addition to the basic elements of education.

The school moved to new buildings on Norton Road in 1786 and it was extended in

60 National School, Norton Green, opened in 1833.

61 Bowesfield Lane School.

62 The High School for Boys which later became Stockton Grammar School.

1810 and 1819. During 1863 it was completely rebuilt in the mock Gothic style at a cost of £3,000 but the school finally closed in 1894.

During the early 19th century a grammar school was opened in West Row and in 1803 a school of industry was set up to provide free education for local girls. Provision for adult education was available at the Mechanics' Institute on Dovecot Street. Opened in 1825, it included reading rooms and arranged study groups.

The Diocese of Durham continued to play an important role in the development of education in Stockton. In 1847 Holy Trinity Higher Grade School was opened on a site adjacent to Yarm Lane. Land had been provided by the bishop of Durham and a directory for 1856 explains that the premises comprised a boys' school, a school of industry and an infants' school. In May 1968 pupils moved to new premises on Upsall Grove at Fairfield. Completed at a cost of £74,000, the school was officially opened by a former pupil, Viscount Mills. The old school buildings were demolished during May 1970.

Legislation in the 1870s and 1880s resulted in completion of several new schools in Stockton. Forster's Education Act received the Royal Assent on 9 August 1870 and within four months the town's first school Board was elected. Mill Lane School opened on 8 October 1873.

63 Former Higher Grade School on Nelson Terrace which was used in its final years by the College of Art—viewed from the cleared area of Cobden Street.

The requirements of further legislation—including Balfour's Education Act of 1902—and the development of housing away from the town centre meant more school buildings. Richard Hind School opened on 14 January 1913 and operated as an elementary school until January 1922 when it was converted to a selective central school. A central block of buildings was opened on 18 January 1927 and this included a handicrafts room and physics laboratory (shared between the boys' and girls' sections). In August 1931 an additional form of pupils was enrolled and the nearby St Peter's Hall was used as a teaching base.

A feature of the school's achievements was its sporting success. Though it had no playing fields nor sports facilities on the site, the boys' school won many honours including the Durham County Cup final (soccer) on 10 May 1937. This represented the first victory by a team in south-east Durham and there was further victory in the same competition in 1952. The school closed when war broke out in 1939 but reopened in November of that year with air raid shelters in the school yard. Further teaching rooms were added in 1949 and 1955 and in the mid-1950s the boys' and girls' departments amalgamated. The school closed in December 1978 and moved to a new site on Harrowgate Lane (as Bishopsgarth School) in January 1979. In the early 1980s the Richard Hind school buildings were demolished and replaced by 'starter homes'.

Other schools completed during the inter-war period include Frederick Nattrass, built in the early 1920s to serve the Blue Hall and

64 *(Left)* Alderman Richard Hind, J.P.C.C., after whom the school was named.

65 *(Below)* Richard Hind Secondary Technical School staff, 1962.

Norton areas, and Newham Grange opened on 6 November 1936 by Alderman W. Newton. The school was built on a double quadrangular plan covering a 10-acre site, and a teaching staff of 10 were responsible for 360 scholars.

Alderman William Newton's services to local government were recognised when a new girls' school was named after him. Work started on a five and a half acre site, adjacent to Junction Road, in February 1938 and Alderman Newton performed the official opening on 26 August 1939.

Some schemes spanned the war years. Preparatory work on the new Grangefield Grammar School site (on Oxbridge Lane) began in 1939 but it was not until Friday 2 November 1951 that the buildings were officially opened by Alderman J. Alderson J.P. (This school was the successor to an earlier building in Prince Regent Street. Opened in 1896, Nelson Terrace Higher Grade School became Stockton Secondary School in 1906, then Stockton Secondary School for Boys and Girls in 1915, and latterly Stockton Secondary Grammar School from 1944. The building was demolished in the final months of 1984.) In 1973 the premises became the Grange School under the comprehensive system, and some twenty years later it was renamed Grangefield School.

One of the town's best-known educational institutions—and for many years one of its landmarks on Yarm Road—was the Queen Victoria High School. The origins of the school can be traced to a meeting in the Borough Hall on 19 September 1882 when it was agreed that a high school should be established in Stockton. Later in the year a company was formed under the name Stockton High School Limited and on 1 May 1883 the first nine pupils attended school at Cleveland House on Bowesfield Lane. Three years later the school moved to premises on Yarm Road and numbered among the third year pupils in 1890 was Laura Smithson, who went on to become a well-known actress.

In March 1901 a site was purchased on the corner of Yarm Road and Cranbourne Terrace. Building work began in 1904 and the school was officially opened by Princess Henry of Battenberg (youngest daughter of Queen Victoria) on 19 September 1905. By the end of the First World War there were 174 pupils on roll, many of whom gained places at Oxford and Cambridge Universities. There was yet another change of premises when the school

66 Queen Victoria High School for Girls on Yarm Lane.

67 Bailey Street Council Boys' School—winners of the 'Thomas' Football Cup 1928-9.

68 Bluecoats School on Norton Road with St Mary's church in the distance.

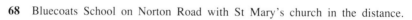

moved to the Teesside High School site during the early 1970s. Buildings on the Yarm Road site were cleared and redeveloped with a public house which perpetuates the name of the school.

Literary and Philosophical Society

A Literary and Philosophical Society was established in 1835 and occupied premises in Dovecot Street. In 1964 the building was sold for £72,500 and funds were allocated towards the cost of constructing the new YMCA block on condition that the Society had the use of rooms in the completed block.

Public Libraries

Stockton's public library service began in 1873 when the town council bought the Masonic Hall (built in 1864) in Wellington Street and adapted it for use as a Free Library. The premises, which included living accommodation for the librarian on the first floor, opened to the public on 2 April 1877. During the 91 years of the library service, until its incorporation in the County Borough of Teesside, there were only three chief librarians: Mr. T. H. Wright, 1877-1919, Miss Eva Scarth, 1919-45, and Mr. G. F. Leighton ALA, 1945-68.

Until 1945 the Wellington Street Library was adequate but during the post-war years increased leisure time and increased stock began to put pressure on resources. Major internal alterations and acquisition of the house next door for use as a book store and staff room did not resolve difficulties and in 1960 the town council approved the scheme in principle.

Further discussion about the site resulted in the choice of location between the parish church and the municipal buildings.

Branch libraries were opened in 1950 at Norton, in 1955 at Roseworth and in 1966 at Fairfield, but it was March 1969 before the fine new central library opened its doors to the public. Completed at a cost of £250,000, its excellent layout and blend of building materials resulted in an award from the Civic Trust.

Chapter Twelve

Places of Care

The problem of caring for sick and needy members of the community has occupied national and local administrators for centuries. Most of the early provision came from Church authorities but during the 19th century an increasing population and rapid industrialisation forced the government to introduce legislation to deal with the situation.

The Poor Law Amendment Act of 1834 addressed the problems of providing for needy members of society. Some two years later—on 4 December 1836—Stockton Union was formed with its 83,774 acres covering sub-districts centred around Stockton, Yarm and Hartlepool. A 'Poor House' had been built on a site in Bishop Street during 1630 and 60 years later the Stockton Dispensary was set up in one of its rooms. When Almshouses were opened in 1816 on the High Street, the dispensary was transferred to this building and medical aid continued to be distributed to sick paupers until 1837.

Stockton Union Workhouse was built in 1851 on Portrack Lane. It had accommodation for 260 inmates and during 1852 a school was opened with the emphasis placed on sewing and knitting for girls and gardening for the boys. In 1861 there were 179 inmates at the Stockton Workhouse, supervised by five staff, and 20 years later a total of nine staff looked after 257 inmates. Periods of industrial depression brought an increase in the number of vagrants and by the 1890s accommodation had been extended

to cope with about 350 inmates. This capacity rose to about 400 places during the early 1900s and, although there was further widespread distress during the 1920s, this total was not increased.

After 1948 Stockton Workhouse was adapted as Portrack Geriatric Hospital and in 1962 it was renamed St Anne's Hospital. Completion of North Tees General Hospital resulted in the demolition of St Anne's in 1977 but a bell which was used for many years at Stockton Workhouse was relocated in the main entrance of North Tees Hospital in 1974.

A surgical hospital was opened close to the town centre on 8 September 1862. It was situated in property on Sugar House Open, a passageway leading from Thistle Green to the Quayside, and had six beds. During the first nine months 23 patients were admitted and 35 outpatients were treated. The busiest night for this tiny hospital is said to have been in 1868 when opposing factions came to blows during an election campaign.

The town's increasing population needed larger premises and on 30 October 1875 the foundation stone of the Stockton and Thornaby Hospital was laid on a site adjacent to Bowesfield Lane. Initial building work was completed at a cost of £9,209 with accommodation for 35 patients—and the first patients were admitted in 1877. The addition of the Fowler Wing in 1890 increased accommodation to 60 beds and in 1926 Princess

69 *(Above right)* People and buildings associated with Stockton and Thornaby hospital.

70 *(Below right)* The opening of Stockton and Thornaby hospital on 23 September 1926 is commemorated on this card.

Queens Nurses Home.

Interior of Women's Ward.

The Marchioness of Londonderry
President of Nursing Association.

Matron & Nursing Staff
of Stockton & Thornaby Hospital.

Frank Brown Esq., J.P.
President of Hospital.

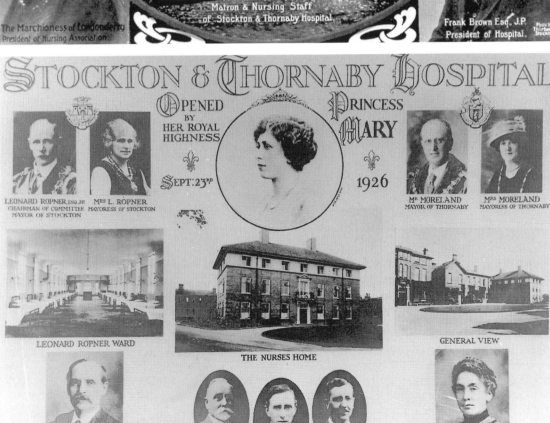

STOCKTON & THORNABY HOSPITAL

OPENED BY HER ROYAL HIGHNESS

PRINCESS MARY

SEPT: 23RD 1926

LEONARD ROPNER, ESQ. J.P.
CHAIRMAN OF COMMITTEE
MAYOR OF STOCKTON

MRS L. ROPNER
MAYORESS OF STOCKTON

MR. MORELAND
MAYOR OF THORNABY

MRS MORELAND
MAYORESS OF THORNABY

LEONARD ROPNER WARD

THE NURSES HOME

GENERAL VIEW

SIR FRANK BROWN, D.L.
PRESIDENT

MR. R. REED, J.P.
HON. TREASURER

MR. A. McLEOD
CONTRACTOR

MR. W. H. DANIELS, A.C.I.S.
SECRETARY

LADY BROWN

71 *(Above)* Demolition of Stockton and Thornaby hospital.

72 *(Left)* Robson Maternity Home on Bowesfield Lane.

73 *(Opposite above)* Opening of North Tees Hospital Maternity Block by the Duchess of Kent.

74 *(Opposite below)* View of North Tees Hospital Maternity Block.

Mary opened extensions costing £70,000. Accommodation now comprised 130 beds, an out-patients' department and a nurses' home, as well as a dispensary and electro-orthopaedic departments. A new casualty department was completed in 1960 but in summer 1974 patients were transferred to the newly completed North Tees Hospital. Buildings were demolished in 1977 and a housing estate was developed on the site two years later. Streets on the new estate are named after wards and individuals associated with the former hospital.

A fever isolation hospital opened on Durham Road in the early 1890s. It became a children's hospital in 1949 and closed in 1974.

The first stage of the new North Tees Hospital was opened at Hardwick in May 1968. This initial phase included maternity and psychiatric units as well as accommodation for 70 day patients. The second phase was completed by the end of 1974.

Many local families have happy memories of the maternity hospital on Bowesfield Lane.

The Robson family's home was given to the corporation in 1919 and for almost fifty years it served as a maternity unit for the town. For much of this time it was supervised by Matron Nixon and some 44,000 babies were born at the home.

Included among the many other people who made a major contribution to Stockton's health service are Mrs. Helen Bott and Dr. G. C. M. M'Gonigle. Mrs. Bott was the wife of the vicar of St John's Church and for over fifty years, starting in 1914, she paid regular visits to needy folk in the poorer sections of Stockton. Her tire-less work for the underprivileged of the town was recognised in 1968 when she became Stockton's first Freewoman. She also received the British Empire Medal and was made a Serving Sister of the St John's Ambulance Brigade.

Dr. M'Gonigle moved to Stockton in 1924 from the Durham County medical staff. Initially appointed as *locum tenens*, he soon took over from Dr. Home as the town's medical officer of health. He went on to achieve national fame as a writer, speaker and practitioner on malnutrition. His book, *Poverty and Public Health*, published in 1938, became a standard

75   View of the North Tees Hospital Maternity block

work and the Ministry of Health tried to secure his part-time services on propaganda relating to malnutrition. Dr. M'Gonigle had a special interest in crippled people—he suffered from lameness himself—and he gave considerable support to Stockton and Thornaby Crippled Children's Guild. He also had special knowledge of orthopaedic work and was instrumental in reducing the number of crippled children in Stockton as well as the town's infant mortality rate. Dr. M'Gonigle was also associated with town planning and housing schemes, such as the clearance of the Thistle Green area, work at the fever hospital on Durham Road, and plans

for Summerhouse School. He died on 30 July 1939 at his home on Norton High Street.

The Almshouses

Bishop Crewe granted a licence for the building of an almshouse and work was completed on a High Street site in 1682. By 1816 the premises had become derelict and George Brown left a bequest of £3,000 for construction of a new building which included accommodation for 36 widows and their families as well as a committee room and dispensary.

This building was sold for £5,000 and the Victoria Buildings were erected on the site. Part

76 Quayside Mission Hall—with a postmark dated 1905.

of the receipts from the sale were used to build a replacement almshouse on Dovecot Street.

Quayside Mission

A familiar landmark on high ground overlooking the river was no.25 The Square. Built as a mansion, it became the 'Quayside Mission Men's Home' during 1906-7 when shipyards lined the adjacent riverside. The building offered clean, respectable and cheap accommodation for shipyard workers who worked long hours and needed to live as close as possible to their place of work. In more recent times it became a home for some fifty long-term homeless men. Much of the surrounding area was cleared but the Mission survived, on the site between the municipal buildings and the quayside, until closure in June 1973. It was demolished during the following year.

Chapter Thirteen

The Sporting Scene

The earliest evidence of organised sporting events in the town dates from the 18th century when a range of blood 'sports' and horse race meetings attracted large numbers of followers. During 'Race Week' in 1742, 50 guineas were on offer in a 'main of cocks' between the gentlemen of Guisborough and Richmondshire. In September 1756 groups of gentlemen from Darlington and Helmsley held a total of 22 cock fights at Stockton. The Darlington group won 12 of the 'battles' and their opponents triumphed in the remaining ten. The usual location for this cruel sport was a cockpit in the centre of Green Dragon Yard, off Finkle Street, and red and black game cocks were specially bred for the contests. Blood sports were made illegal in 1849 and the cockpit was used as a meeting place for Primitive Methodists (before they moved to a new chapel in Maritime Street and, in 1866, to premises on Paradise Row—now known as Church Road). A cooper's workshop then occupied the site of the cockpit before the area was cleared.

Another cruel variation on this sport was throwing at cocks. The aim was to throw stones at the cockerel, knock it down, and then tie up its legs before it could get up from the ground. Bull-baiting was another cruel spectacle in local townships during the 18th and 19th centuries. Crowds of people were attracted to the Coal

77 View of stands and finishing post at Stockton racecourse. Horse racing took place in the Stockton area as early as 1724—at Tibbersley (Billingham) and racing moved to the Mandale course in 1854. The course was named Teesside Park in 1969 but reverted to the name Stockton Racecourse on 29 October 1979 (although the track is actually located at Thornaby). Racing ended in June 1981.

78 Stockton football team—winners of the F.A. Amateur Cup during the 1902-3 season.

79 Stockton football team pictured in 1933.

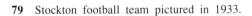

Market, close to Stockton Town Hall, where a bull was tethered to a post and then attacked by dogs, but this sport seems to have ended in 1793 when the bull broke free and escaped.

Horse racing took place on the Carrs—low-lying land across the river from Stockton—in 1724 and at that time Race Week lasted four days. The course covered more than three miles and successful horses ran twice in one day for a prize of 20 guineas. By 1735 women were racing for prizes of a velvet cap and holland smock. Between 1839 and 1845 racing was transferred to a course at Tibbersley (Billingham) and in 1855 the race course was set up on Mandale Marshes (within the original course of the river Tees). This venue became established and the meetings attracted large numbers of racegoers including fashionable and famous members of society who often stayed at

Wynyard Hall before attending the races. Attendances fluctuated but in 1864 a total of 36,000 racegoers attended and in 1917 the total number reached 50,000. During the post-war years the course's fortunes declined and the 1980s brought closure and redevelopment of the site as the Teesside Retail Park.

Stockton cricket club was formed in 1816 and a year later the team played a Yarm side for a prize of £100. During 1840 the club president, Dr. William Richardson, introduced professionalism to the team and by the 1858 season they were recording victories over All England and United England teams. During the 1860s the club's fortunes declined but there was a major success in 1890 when Stockton won the Durham Challenge Cup. Two years later the club moved to its present ground on the corner of Oxbridge Avenue and Grangefield Road.

80 Kevin Brown of Mandale Harriers is pictured in the mayor's parlour after receiving a civic welcome for his achievements during the 1989 season when he won north-east championship medals in the marathon and half marathon events. He also gained his first Great Britain vest.

81   Stockton Sports Centre at Tilery.

Stockton A.F.C.—known as 'The Ancients'—were founder members of the Northern League in 1882 and played at the Victoria Ground in Suffolk Street. During the next 50 years they enjoyed a sustained run of success with eight appearances in the English Amateur Cup Final. The first of these games resulted in a defeat by four goals to one by Old Carthusians. There were successes in 1898 with a 1-0 victory over Eston. They are also recorded in soccer records as the only team to beat West Auckland in the season (during the early 1900s) when their opponents won the first ever World Cup competition.

Other local sporting organisations include athletics, cycling and rowing clubs. The Stockton Athletic and Harriers Confederation held races on a track in the Mount Pleasant area during the 1880s. By the 1920s this venue had become the Belle Vue Greyhound Stadium. The stretch of river below Victoria Bridge has been used for recreational events since the last century. The first rowing regatta took place alongside the Carrs in 1825 and after a gap of many years the event was revived in 1978. Stockton cycling club was formed in 1878 and members placed considerable emphasis on social life, with rides into the countryside and annual dinners. Roller skating also enjoyed popularity in the town. The first rank was housed on premises on Palmerston Street and then in the building on Yarm Lane which had been the Theatre Royal.

Chapter Fourteen

The 18th Century

The 1700s brought progress and expansion to most aspects of Stockton's development and this is probably best illustrated by the number of prominent buildings that were erected. Plans for a parish church, replacing the chapel of ease, got underway in 1710 and the completed building was consecrated on 21 August 1712. An Act of Parliament dated 1711 created the parish of Stockton on Tees which was separate from Norton. In 1735 the Town House was built on the orders of Stockton Corporation and during 1768 John Shout paid for the construction of a Doric Column to replace an earlier wooden cross.

In the early months of 1766 a barn in Green Dragon Yard was converted into the town's first theatre and the 1780s saw completion of a grammar school in West Row (1785) and the opening of buildings associated with the Blue Coat Charity School (1786).

By the mid-18th century the port of Stockton was prospering and completion of vessels such as *The Preston*, 1776-7 and *The Bellona* at Pye and Haw's Yards, heralded a boom period for ship building. This expansion in trade brought a need for improved communications and in March 1762 an Act of Parliament was obtained 'for building a bridge across the river Tease, at or near unto, and instead of the ferry now used as a passage over the river'. Foundations of the toll bridge were laid on 23 August 1764 and the bridge opened in 1771.

Public works projects during the early 1700s included the completion of causeways on the High Street in 1717 and, soon afterwards, paving of the whole of the main thoroughfare.

An increasing population and growth of the business and commercial sector produced a number of eminent personalities. Edmund

Harvey, a pewterer by trade, was born in the town in 1698 and set up an early 'ragged school' at his workshop on Finkle Street. The premises provided basic education for boys, and later, girls, until his death in 1781. He also had the foresight to put forward plans for 'cuts' in the course of the river Tees at Thornaby and Portrack but it was more than forty years before the first of his schemes was carried out.

Born in the town in 1751, Thomas Sheraton was educated locally and then employed as a journeyman cabinet-maker where he would learn the skills needed to build furniture and plan ships' ward rooms. He also had strong Baptist convictions and these resulted in the publication of a religious tract, *A Scriptural Illustration of the Doctrine of Regeneration*, in 1782.

The Stockton district offered few openings for Sheraton's work and he moved to London in about 1790. Much of the material contained in his first two London publications must have been compiled in Stockton and these included *Design for Furniture* and, in 1791, *The Cabinet Maker and Upholsterers Drawing Book*. In 1793 Thomas Sheraton's father died and he probably attended the funeral in his home town because an engraving of the north end of Stockton High Street, printed locally, appeared in 1794. During 1795 he lived at a number of addresses in London before settling at 106 Wardour Street to concentrate on the design of furniture making. Wording on his work card explained that he taught 'perspective, architecture and ornaments', made designs for cabinet makers, and sold all kinds of drawing books.

Sheraton spent the first couple of years of the 19th century in Stockton where he was minister of the Baptist congregation and during the following year he published *Cabinet*

82   High Street viewed from the north with the parish church and Town House dominating this central sector.

Dictionary. In 1804 he began work on *The Cabinet Maker, Upholsterer and General Artists' Encyclopaedia* which was to appear in 125 monthly parts, but before long overwork began to put a strain on Sheraton's output— only 30 parts of the encyclopaedia were published. During the final months of his life designs became more and more eccentric and he died 'of an phrenitis' (inflammation of the brain) on 22 October 1806. It was some forty years later before the significance of Sheraton's work was appreciated. The most distinguishing feature of Sheraton's cabinets was the swan-necked pediment surrounding the cornice, and the theme of his design work was that successful simplicity is more desirable than the excess of ornamentation.

Included among other Stockton-born personalities who made their way to the capital for different reasons are Brass Crosby and Margaret Nicholson. Brass Crosby was born at Stockton on 8 May 1725 and worked in the office of a Sunderland solicitor before moving to London where he served for a number of years as an attorney. Between 1758 and 1764 he held offices such as councillor, sheriff and alderman, and then from 1768-74 Crosby was M.P. for Hamilton. On 29 September 1770 Brass Crosby was elected Lord Mayor of London and he soon became involved in a struggle with the House of Commons over press coverage of parliamentary proceedings. This resulted in imprisonment in the Tower of London but he was released, amid great popular rejoicing, on 8 May 1771. In future there was to be no attempt to restrain publication of parliamentary debates. Brass Crosby died on 14 February 1773 after a short illness. An obelisk was placed in the centre of St George's Circus, Blackfriars Road, in honour of his year as Lord Mayor.

Margaret Nicholson was born at Stockton in 1750 and spent her early working life in the town as a housemaid. She moved to London and lived for three years in lodgings on the corner of Wigmore Street, Marylebone, where she made a living by taking in needlework. During 1786 she sent a petition to the Privy Council on the subject of pretenders and usurpers to the throne but it received no attention. Soon afterwards, on 2 August, Margaret Nicholson was among a crowd of people at the garden entrance to St James'

Palace as King George III arrived back from Windsor. She presented a paper to him and then attempted to stab him with an old ivory-handled dessert knife. The knife passed through the waistcoat and bent against his skin but she was disarmed and led away to detention. Among her belongings in Marylebone letters to prominent people were discovered and in these she claimed to have a right to the throne.

On 8 August she appeared before the Privy Council and two doctors certified her to be insane. She was committed to Bethleham (or Bedlam) Hospital and died there on 14 May 1828.

The Writers

Joseph Reed was born in Stockton in March 1723 and educated briefly at Appleby and then in his home town. His main interest was in writing dramatic poetry and in August 1744 a poem, *In Imitation of the Scottish dialect, on the death of Mr Pope*, was published in *Gentleman's Magazine*. During the following year his first play, a farce entitled *The Superannuated Gallant*, was performed at Newcastle.

In the late 1750s he moved his family and his rope-making business to London and in July 1758 a tragedy by Reed, *Madrigal and Trulletta*, was performed at Covent Garden Theatre. It was badly received by contemporary critics but Reed was undaunted and replied in a pamphlet entitled, *A Sop in the Pan for a Physical Critic*, published in 1759. He had much more success with a farce, *The Register Office*, which had a good run at the Drury Lane Theatre in April 1761. Its strongest appeal was probably its characters who included Margery Moorpoot from *Canny Yatton under Roseberry*. A tragedy, *Dido*, also enjoyed brief success in March 1767 until a disagreement with the manager of Drury Lane ended its run and in *The Retort Courteous or a Candid Appeal*, published in 1787, Reed attacked the theatre manager for not receiving the play. *Tom Jones*, a comic opera adapted from Fielding's work, also enjoyed a fair measure of success and his last acted play was *The Imposters or a Cure for Credulity* which was first performed at the Covent Garden Theatre on 19 March 1776. Joseph Reed died on 15 August 1787 and was buried at Bunhill Fields.

Joseph Ritson was born at Stockton on 2 October 1752 and educated in the town before joining the practice of Ralph Bradley,

conveyancer. He soon developed an interest in literature, published pamphlets and befriended writers and musicians. In the late 1770s Ritson joined a conveyancing firm and during 1780 he began his own business in Gray's Inn. He continued to further his conveyancing career but away from business Joseph Ritson had a consuming interest in ancient literature, poetry and drama. He became one of the earliest collectors of local verse and published a number of northern collections during the 1780s and early 1790s, but eccentricity resulted in controversies with other writers. Many of these were conducted in the columns of the *Gentleman's Magazine* and during the mid-1780s he successfully demonstrated that 'John Pinkerton's Select Scottish Ballads' was mostly made up of forgeries.

He made frequent visits to Stockton and in 1781 he issued *The Stockton Jubilee* or *Shakespeare in all his Glory*, a witty attack on the senior citizens of his home town. For a number of years he supported the Jacobite cause and, following a visit to Paris in 1791, Ritson gave firm backing to a Republican calendar. During the late 1790s he was faced with nervous troubles and financial problems but he lived until 23 September 1803 when he died at the house of a friend in Hoxton.

Sea-going Men

A number of local men were drawn to a maritime career in times of commercial expansion and armed confrontation with the Dutch and French navies. Captain Jonathan Fowler spent most of his sea-going days in the service of the Hudson's Bay Company and during several expeditions to the north Atlantic he and Captain William Christopher distinguished themselves during clashes with French forces. Captain Fowler died in June 1790, aged 57, and Captain Christopher died at Newcastle in 1797.

Christopher Allison distinguished himself in 1758 when, as master of *The Adventurer*, he captured a French privateer in the English Channel. He died in his home town of Stockton on 11 July 1808, aged 87.

Sir Thomas Bertie was born at Stockton, to George and Frances Hoar on 3 July 1758, and began a long and illustrious career in the navy in October 1773. During his time on board HMS *Seahorse* he was a messmate and friend of Nelson and Troubridge. In 1777 he was promoted to the rank of lieutenant and spent most of the following four years in the West Indies aboard *The Monarch*, where he took part in several engagements against the French before returning to England in 1783. On 20 May 1788 Captain Hoar married Catherine Dorothy Bertie and adopted her surname. During the 1790s he commanded several vessels during warfare against the French and was commended for his achievements in evacuating *The Texel*, and at the Battle of Copenhagen. He was commander of *The Bellona* during the blockade of the Spanish Fleet that preceded peace in 1802 and, after further outstanding successes in the early 1800s, he was promoted to the rank of Rear Admiral of the Blue Squadron in 1808. His last commands were in the Baltic area where he organised blockades of the islands of Zealand and adjacent channels. On 10 February 1810 he resigned his command because of ill health but further promotions culminated in him achieving the rank of Admiral on 28 May 1825. He died soon afterwards at his brother's home in Hampshire on 14 June 1825.

Chapter Fifteen

John Walker—Inventor of the friction match

Born on 29 May 1781 at 104 High Street, Stockton, he was educated in the town—probably at the Grammar School in West Row—where he became very knowledgeable about chemistry, botany and mineralogy. After leaving school he was apprenticed to a local surgeon, Mr. Watson Alcock, and after further studies at Durham he moved to London and qualified as a surgeon.

On his return to Stockton, John Walker gave up his career as a surgeon and joined a firm of druggists. He worked in Durham and York before establishing a business at 59 High Street, Stockton, in the early months of 1819. He continued to experiment in order to find means of igniting a suitable compound by a single friction match but it was not until 1826 that he found the answer. During that year he produced a flame on three-inch splints which had been dipped in a chemical mixture and the first recorded sale, according to his day book, appears on 7 April 1827. By 23 September 1829, sales of 23,206 friction lights had been recorded in his day book. They were sold for one shilling per hundred (plus two pence for a case) along with a small piece of glass paper which was used to create the surfaces needed for ignition by friction.

John Walker moved to a house overlooking the green area close to the parish church and in February 1858 he retired from business without patenting his invention. He died at his home in May 1859 and is buried in Norton churchyard. His achievements are celebrated by a pew end in the parish church and a commemorative bust at the southern end of Stockton High Street in John Walker Square.

83. The commemorative bust to John Walker in John Walker Square at the southern end of the High Street.

Chapter Sixteen

The Coming of Steam

Stockton's expansion in trade during the 18th century prompted calls for improved transport systems in the locality and in September 1810 the cut in the Mandale Loop of the river was officially opened. It was at the celebratory banquet for this event that proposals were put forward for a canal or railway to link Stockton to the south Durham coalfield (via Darlington). Schemes for a canal were surveyed, costed and eventually dismissed as too expensive before a group of local businessmen led by Edward Pease put forward proposals for a railway. The line was authorised by an Act of Parliament on 19 April 1821 and in August of that year George Stephenson accepted the appointment of engineer for the project. The first rail was laid near St John's Well, Stockton, on 22 May 1822 and some three years later the proprietors announced that the line from Witton Park Colliery to Stockton would be formally opened on 27 September 1825.

Locomotion No.1 was built at Newcastle-on-Tyne and transported in separate parts, on three trolleys, to Aycliffe crossing at Heighington. Here it was assembled and placed on the rails a few days before the official ceremony. On the opening day a total of 38 carriages were linked to the engine and tender, and many more than the 300 ticket holders clambered aboard the carriages. The procession covered the eight and three quarter miles to Darlington in 65 minutes and, after stopping to take on water and more passengers, the cavalcade moved on to Stockton past crowds of cheering onlookers. It took three hours and seven minutes to cover the 12 miles from Darlington to Stockton and, as the procession reached the riverside, seven 18-pound guns fired a salute three times. Thomas Meynell's Band of Music, from Yarm, played the national anthem and then accompanied directors, dignitaries and their friends to a dinner in Stockton Town Hall.

After the opening day passenger traffic was carried by horse-drawn coaches for the next eight years, with available locomotives being reserved for freight, but the line claims its place in railway history as the first steam-worked public railway conveying traffic for reward.

The permanent way was made up of a mixture of cast iron and malleable iron

84 The *George and Dragon* at Yarm. The meeting of promoters of the Stockton-Darlington Railway took place in the building on 12 February 1820.

85 *(Above)* Buildings adjacent to Bridge Road, Stockton. The first turf was cut at this location in 1821 to start work on the Stockton-Darlington railway line. The buildings have traditionally been known as the ticket office for the Stockton-Darlington railway.

STOCKTON AND DARLINGTON RAILWAY
COACHES.

ST. HELEN'S AUCKLAND TO DARLINGTON.			DARLINGTON TO ST. HELEN'S AUCKLAND.		
First Trip	..	at half-past 8 o'clock.	First Trip	..	at half-past 8 o'clock.
Second do	.. ..	at 1 "	Second do	.. ..	at 1 "
Third do	.. ..	at 6 "	Third do	.. ..	at 6 "

DARLINGTON TO STOCKTON.			STOCKTON TO DARLINGTON.		
Merchandize Train at ½ past 6 o'clock.			First Class Train at 10 m. bef. 8 o'clock.		
First Class	do	at ½ past 9 "	Merchandize do at 10 m. bef. 9 "		
Merchandize	do	at 11 "	First Class	do at 20 m. past 12 "	
First Class	do	at 2 "	Merchandize do at 20 m. past 2 "		
Merchandize	do	at 4 "	First Class	do at 20 m. past 5 "	
First Class	do	at 7 "	Merchandize do at half-past 6 "		

An Omnibus from the Fighting Cocks to Middleton, meets the First Class Trains.
The Evening Coaches from the South arrive in Darlington in time for the 7 o'clock Train to Stockton and Middlesbro'.

STOCKTON TO MIDDLESBROUGH.				MIDDLESBROUGH TO STOCKTON.			
First	Trip	.. at	8 o'clock.	*First	Trip	.. half-past	7 o'clock.
Second	do	.. at	9 "	Second	do	.. half-past	8 "
*Third	do	.. at	10 "	Third	do	.. half-past	9 "
Fourth	do	.. at	11 "	Fourth	do	.. half-past	10 "
Fifth	do	.. half-past 12 "		*Fifth	do	.. at	12 "
Sixth	do	.. half-past 1 "		Sixth	do	.. at	1 "
*Seventh	do	.. half-past 2 "		Seventh	do	.. at	2 "
Eighth	do	.. half-past 3 "		Eighth	do	.. at	3 "
Ninth	do	.. half-past 4 "		Ninth	do	.. at	4 "
Tenth	do	.. half-past 5 "		*Tenth	do	.. at	5 "
Eleventh	do	.. half-past 6 "		Eleventh	do	.. at	6 "
*Twelfth	do	.. half-past 7 "		Twelfth	do	.. at	7 "

* Are in connexion with the First Class Trains to and from Darlington.
TICKETS must be taken at least Five Minutes before the Trains start.
NO SMOKING ALLOWED IN ANY OF THE COMPANY'S COACHES.

MARKET COACH:
A Coach and Cattle Carriage will leave St. Helen's Auckland on Mondays, at half-past 6 o'clock, and Shildon at 7 in the Morning.
HORSES, CARRIAGES, AND CATTLE, CAREFULLY CONVEYED FROM STOCKTON AND ST. HELEN'S AUCKLAND TO DARLINGTON.
Horse, 2s.; Gig, 2s.; or Horse and Gig, 3s.; Four-wheeled Carriages, 5s.; or with Two Horses, 5s. Horned Cattle, 1s. 6d. each; Sheep, 4d. each, or 5s. per Score; Dogs, 1s each.

Railway Office, Darlington, May 14th, 1840.

86 *(Left)* Details of departure times of the Stockton and Darlington railway coaches dated 1840

87 View of Stamp Street and Stockton railway station.

88 Scenes connected with railway achievements feature on this centenary postcard of 1925.

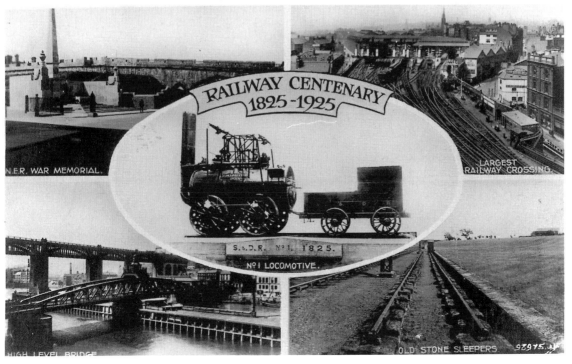

89 *(Above)* Stockton railway station.

90 *(Left)* Christopher Tennant, a Stockton gentleman and generous subscriber to the Stockton-Darlington railway project of the early 1820s. He moved to Hartlepool in 1832 and was instrumental in establishing the Clarence Railway and early industrial development up to his death in 1839.

fish-bellied rails supported on stone sleepers and the track, at first only a single line, was duplicated in 1831. A year earlier, the eastern terminus of the line was extended from Stockton to deeper water at Middlesbrough by the construction of a suspension bridge. Coal shipments to 'Port Darlington'—as this new venture at Middlesbrough was known—set the scene for the phenomenal growth of Stockton's near neighbour and rival that took place in the second half of the 19th century.

The introduction of steampower into sea-going vessels took place slowly during the mid-1800s. At first steamships were limited to river and coastal trade owing to the limited capacity of early marine engines. As reliability and efficiency improved, the use of steam engines became more widespread and by the late 1890s the superiority of steam over sail was virtually complete.

At about the same time, steam tramways were being constructed on local thoroughfares. On 22 October 1881 the Steam Tramway began operations from Brewery Bank, South Stockton (Thornaby), to Norton Green along a single-track route, with passing places, and branch lines to St Peter's parish church on Yarm Road and Stockton railway station. A particularly busy

91 Fire engine dated 1888. The town's fire station was situated in West Row.

passing place was at Grey Horse Corner—the junction of Yarm Lane and the High Street—and the steam engines caused problems along the route for horse cabbies when frightened horses bolted causing accidents. The track was relaid in 1897 with a gauge of three feet six inches, and the new system, installed by the Imperial Tramway Company of Bristol, was opened to the public on 16 July 1898. The last tram to run on this system made its journey on 31 December 1931.

Chapter Seventeen

1900-45

The early years of this century brought a number of notable building schemes. Corporation Quay was constantly in the news and in July 1900 there were plans for extensions to the existing 650ft.-long wharf as tonnage dealt with since 1895 had increased from 81,528 tons per year to 113,194 in 1900. Robinson's New Coliseum was opened to the public during the first week in May 1901 (replacing the former building destroyed by fire in 1899) and among new churches completed in the Edwardian period were the church and schools built by primitive Methodists in Norton Road (opened on

17 October 1901) and the Baptist Tabernacle on Wellington Street (opened on 1 June 1903).

There were hard times for local people during 1908, with widespread poverty and unemployment, but on 20 October 1909 a meeting of Stockton Board of Guardians heard that the amount of outdoor relief paid during the past fortnight totalled £395 12s.—representing a decrease of £10 8s. 9d. from the corresponding fortnight of the previous year. The town's gloomy prospects had been further brightened by the opening of the Castle Theatre (on 31 July 1908). Press reports talked of a 'Charming House

92   View of Yarm Lane in the early 1900s.

93 Frontage and gable, with ornate feature showing the date '1909' on the former police station.

94 Cattle market on Church Road. The site is now covered by the municipal buildings.

95 Construction work on the berths at Furness Shipyard, Haverton Hill. The project was completed in 1917 by women and older menfolk as most of the local male workers were involved in hostilities on the continent.

of Dramatic Art' and the new theatre and business premises were built by North Eastern Brewery Company. Another 'Handsome new building'—the Stockton Police Court—was opened as the new police station on Church Row during March 1910.

Travellers on the Victoria Bridge watched the completion of one of the district's best known landmarks during the early months of 1912. The new grain silo at the Cleveland Flour Mills site on the south bank of the Tees had a total height of 130 ft. and included 15 bins which could hold a total of 3,700 tons of wheat when full.

The early months of 1914 brought calls for river-based developments at Stockton. On 26 February the *Great City* was launched from the yard of Messrs. Ropner and Sons. Weighing 10,000 tons, she was, according to the local press, 'the largest vessel yet launched on the higher reaches of the Tees'. During the following months there were renewed calls for development of the river at Stockton but the

outbreak of war in August refocused priorities. Soon after the outbreak of hostilities, Belgian refugees were arriving in the area and injured troops were moved to local centres for treatment and convalescence. In December 1914 the horrors of modern warfare were brought home as nearby Hartlepool was blasted by German battlecruisers. The later stages of the war were brightened with the news that a Stockton man, Sgt. Edward Cooper, had won the Victoria Cross during the Third Battle of Ypres on 16 August 1917. He received a rapturous reception on his arrival at Stockton railway station a month later (on 17 September 1917). During 1918 he was promoted to the rank of second lieutenant and, after rejoining his battalion, fighting ended on the same ground as it had begun at the start of hostilities.

Following demobilisation in 1919 Edward Cooper married the young lady that he had courted (by letter) since 1917 and returned to employment with the Stockton Cooperative

96 *(Above)* Employees of Imperial Tramways photographed at the tram depot in March 1910.

97 *(Right)* Molten iron is poured at Parkfield Foundry as employees look on.

Society as under-manager of the fruit department.

During the Sescond World War, Edward Cooper was in charge of the Thornaby Company of the Home Guard and assumed the rank of major. For 20 years, between 1949 and 1968,

Major Cooper served as a magistrate and on 24 July 1985 he was given the Freedom of Stockton. He died less than four weeks later on 19 August 1985.

Violence returned to the streets of the north east in summer 1921 when Sinn Fein gangs

98 Advertisement for one of the town's major employers—Head Wrightson and Co. Ltd—during the first half of the 20th century.

99 Advertisement for Head Wrightson and Co. Ltd. indicating its wide range of products and world-wide reputation.

100 Construction work on the Teesdale Ironworks at Thornaby-on-Tees. Many of the workforce travelled by ferry from Stockton to this location.

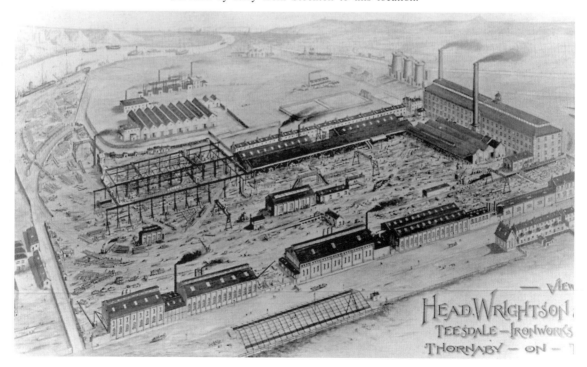

101 Sir Robert Ropner. Born in Magdeburg, Germany, in 1838, he arrived in the north east in 1857. During 1874 he founded a shipping company which became the country's foremost tramp fleet. The family moved to Preston Hall in October 1882.

102 Diamond wedding photograph of the Ropner family at Preston Hall in 1918. Lady Ropner died in 1921 and Sir Robert became seriously ill and died in 1924.

attacked industrial targets. Press reports ran headlines such as 'Fire Gangs Mad Orgy, Shipyards, Railways, Cinemas, and Sawmill attacked, North East Coast Ablaze' (23 May 1921), and among a whole series of incidents a water main close to Long Newton was blown up and the premises of Messrs. Forster, Brotherton and Company (timber merchants) in Bridge Road, Stockton were destroyed by fire. There was a sequel to these events on 3 June when four men were arrested in the Grove Hill district of Middlesbrough. They fired on police before being overpowered and were found to be in possession of a quantity of explosives.

Much of Stockton's older housing had become unfit for human habitation and during the late 1920s and early 1930s large sectors were cleared. During 1928 much of the Thistle Green area was condemned as unfit and rased to the ground. Landmarks such as Burton House

103   *(Left)* Housing on the quayside behind castle wharf.

104   *(Below)* The building at Newtown Corner bears the date 1897. Housing spread along this sector of land between Durham Road and Bishopton Road during the early part of this century.

Newtown Corner,   Stockton-on-Tees   No. 685

105 Cab ranks and electric trams at the southern end of the High Street. This card is postmarked 1902.

106 South end of the High Street with motor vehicles, bicycles, horsedrawn cab and electric tram illustrating different forms of transport.

107 An important occasion in Stockton, the Hirings took place on two Wednesdays before old May Day and two Wednesdays before Martinmas Day. Farm-workers were hired and the arrangement (which usually lasted for six months) was sealed with a 'Hiring Penny'—one shilling.

108 South end of the High Street at the junction with Castlegate, Bridge Road and Yarm Lane. The Empire Cinema (formerly the Castle Theatre) and Barry's provide contrasts in building styles and functions.

were demolished as part of this scheme, but shopping premises along the High Street were drawing large numbers of customers. There were claims that Stockton was one of the cheapest shopping centres in the north of England—with success based on value for money shopping and an efficient bus service. Slum clearance schemes again made the news in 1934—'Stockton's New War On Slums. Decent Homes For The Poor. Riverside Hovels Marked For Demolition. Unfit To Live In' (5 January 1934).

There was further town centre redevelopment, and a boost to local employment prospects, with work on an important new road. Plans were announced in summer 1934— 'Stockton's New Road. 2½ Year Task. Tentacle Which May Bring More Trade. £135,000 Boon To Army of Workless. The new highway is to run along Church Row, Paradise Row and Maritime Street across L.N.E.R. and through Portrack to a point on the Haverton Hill Road near to the new road leading to Tees Bridge. It

109 Wren's corn mill—near Brown's Bridge on Durham Road—photographed in 1910.

will be one of the biggest schemes the Corporation has entered upon for some years.'

The opening weeks of 1935 brought better news on the industrial front with reports that rapid progress was being made on the new coal oil plant at Billingham. A £225,000 factory was under construction on the 40-acre site and there were prospects of employment for 1,500 local workers. Later the same month there was encouraging news about another local company—F. Hills and Sons Ltd.—'Stockton Firm Expanding. Biggest Window Factory In The World. Bold Policy. Employment For More Men' (28 January 1935). However the 1930s brought the beginning of the end for shipping at Stockton. In February 1935 press reports noted that the port of Stockton had declined since the pre-war years. During 1934 approximately 420 vessels had visited the Stockton region of the Tees and, of the 12 wharves in the port, one belonged to Stockton Corporation (8 February 1935).

During the early months of the Second World War it was a case of normality in most aspects of Stockton's day-to-day life. Stockton market carried on business as usual—in spite of sandbags—and schools were to reopen during October 1939. There were plans for 4,000 public shelters in the High Street area and another 3,000 close to traffic routes. By early October 1939, a total of 5,500 Anderson shelters had been ordered—with 4,000 already delivered.

During the summer months of 1940 there were a number of air raids on Thornaby Aerodrome (6 and 8 June, 6 and 24 September) and on the Norton, Portrack and Haverton areas (July and August). The raid on 25/26 August caused damage to properties on the Thornaby side of the river and to premises (including the *Vane Arms*) on the east side of the High Street. Gas pipes under Victoria Bridge were ruptured and cast-iron balustrades on the Thornaby side of the structure still bear shrapnel holes caused during the raid.

Cinemas continued to show all-time favourites such as Walt Disney's *Pinocchio*, and *Rebecca* starring Laurence Olivier and Joan Fontaine at the Regal during the first two weeks of November 1940. There were encouraging reports about the town's Corporation Quay in mid November with plans to install new cranes and railway sidings in response to increased trade at the wharf, and the year closed with the forwarding of a £5,000 cheque from the townspeople of Stockton, Thornaby and Billingham to Lord Beaverbrook towards the cost of buying a Spitfire.

Air raids during 1941 resulted in the first civilian deaths in Stockton. At about midnight on 11/12 May bombs were dropped close to St Peter's Church (Yarm Road) and the Oxbridge, Bowesfield and Hartburn Avenue areas. A number of properties were demolished and several people lost their lives. At about the same time (9 May 1941) it was announced that Kelly's ferry was to reopen. It had recently stopped operations but was to be reinstated at a cost of £200-£300 as an alternative river crossing during war time.

The later war years were characterised by further air raids—mainly targetted at the Billingham and Stockton districts. During the war years a total of 21 civilians were killed in Stockton (with a further 15 at Billingham) and 194 houses were destroyed in the town with damage to almost 2,000 other properties. Fund-raising schemes and morale-boosting events featured prominently and, as plans were laid for celebrating the end of hostilities in the summer of 1945, local folk were celebrating a return to normal living with the second annual show of the Stockton Agricultural and Horticultural Society at Ropner Park on 18 August 1945.

Chapter Eighteen

High Street Scenes

The quality and variety of shops along both sides of the wide main street attracted customers from large sectors of north Yorkshire and south Durham.

110 Stockton High Street premises in the late 1860s.

111   A water cart and horse and dray are pictured in the High Street in 1903.

112   The layout of the northern end of the High Street is seen clearly on this view from
the upper level of the Town House.

113 The Misses Ward clothing and hosiery business on Stockton High Street, photographed in the early 1900s.

114 A street vendor in Stockton High Street, photographed in 1910.

115 The northern end of the High Street with the war memorial, Victoria Buildings and Town House
forming a background to the tram car.

116 The junction of Bishopton Lane and High Street.

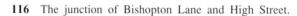

117 Motor buses and charabancs at the southern end of the High Street during the inter-war years.

118 A familiar figure at Stockton market, Jack Roberts, who operated the weighing machine for over fifty years. The market was 675 years old in 1985.

119   Victoria Buildings. They were demolished in 1964 and replaced by Lindsay House.

Chapter Nineteen

Modern Times

As the period of post-war regeneration and development got underway, Stockton's Corporation Quay was again making news:

Stockton Quay's Fine Feat ... The quay which has the distinction of being the first rail-connected wharf in the world, has modern luffing cranes fitted with the latest type of grabs ... 'Lysander IV' was unloaded of nearly 2,500 tons of ore between 7am Friday and noon Saturday ... for practical purposes 2¾ shifts or 18 hours ...

(*Evening Gazette*, 23 July 1946).

Housing development during the 1940s brought new estates at Ragworth, Fairfield, Greens Lane, Newham Grange and Roseworth while Stockton's High Street was given a facelift in summer 1950 with replacement of the wide cobbled surface by a dual carriageway.

The town gained major educational institutions during 1950-1. Work started on the £1,250,000 project to build Stockton and Billingham Technical College premises at Billingham and Fairfield in March 1950 while Grangefield Grammar School was officially

120 Properties on Church Road. No. 70 *(on the left)* dates from the early 19th century and no. 72, now Gloucester House, was originally two three-storey 18th-century houses. The buildings were renovated by Stockton Council during the 1980s.

121 Bridge Road and the approach to Victoria Bridge. One of the town's busiest thoroughfares is pictured before recent redevelopment.

opened on 3 November 1951. Local press reports commented on the final phase of building work—'Life at the Ghost School next month ... the boys department of the new grammar school in Oxbridge Avenue, first projected in 1927 and left half completed in 1939 will be opened next month. The girls will move in during September or October'.

Preston Hall, former home of the Ropner family, was opened as a museum on 3 June 1953 and in recent years it has been developed as one of the north east's major leisure and recreational venues (*see* chapter on Open Spaces).

Residential development during the 1950s included blocks of three-storey flats at Portrack—first opened on 28 July 1955—and houses at Newtown and Hardwick where the town's mayor, Councillor P. J. Milne, got building work underway on 15 December 1956. Press reports suggested that 'Stockton's Hardwick Will Be A Town Itself' (*Evening Gazette*, 16 December 1956)—with plans for a total of 10,000 houses and amenities which included a health centre, shops and schools.

Stockton was included on the itinerary when H.M. Queen Elizabeth and H.R.H. Prince Philip visited Teesside on 4 June 1956 and their stay in the town incorporated an eight-mile tour of the locality.

During the 1960s Stockton gained impressive buildings in the Church Road area. The Municipal Buildings were opened in 1961 at a cost of £200,000 (extensions costing £2 million were occupied in mid-April 1988), the central library opened in March 1969 (see section on Places of Learning), and on the opposite side of Church Road the swimming baths and YMCA building were completed. The YMCA building was opened by Queen Elizabeth on 12 March 1968 and in August of the same year the new swimming baths were opened at a cost of £300,000. (The original baths, on nearby Baths Lane, had been opened in 1859.)

Stockton's days as a port ended on 23 August 1967 when a vessel named *Dora Reith* left Corporation Quay. On 1 April 1968 Stockton became one of the six authorities that formed the County Borough of Teesside.

122 The tower of Debenham's store dominates the scene close to Prince Regent Street after clearance of housing.

123 Market day and construction work on the Castle Centre is underway during 1970-1.

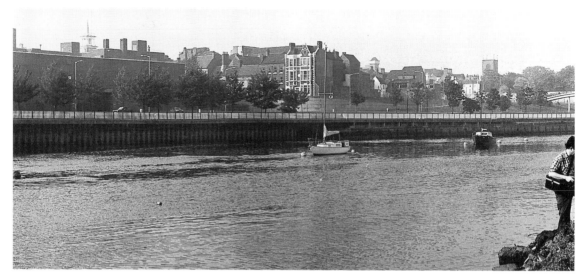

124   Redevelopment of the riverside at Stockton, viewed from the opposite bank.

125   The Masonic Hall on Wellington Street overshadows housing redevelopment in the early 1980s.

During the early days of June 1970 work started on the £5-million redevelopment scheme of Stockton High Street's east side. The foundation stone for the Castle Centre was laid on 10 March 1971 by Alderman G. T. Thornton.

Further local government changes took effect on 1 April 1974 when Teesside went out of existence. It was replaced by Cleveland County, made up of four districts: Hartlepool, Stockton-on-Tees, Middlesbrough and Langbaurgh.

126 Post-war housing development on Stockton's north eastern fringe, Portrack flats.

127 Fully modernised and energy efficient council houses on the Clarences estate at Port Clarence.

The 150th Anniversary of the opening of the Stockton and Darlington railway was celebrated on 27 September 1975. H.R.H. the Duke of Edinburgh visited official events at Preston Park before travelling to Darlington where he opened the North Road Railway Museum. Ten years later the town celebrated three more anniversaries. Stockton market was 675 years old, the parish church celebrated 750 years, and the town hall 250 years.

Since 1986 Stockton has seen several redevelopment programmes. During that year a £1.2-million scheme for new and restored buildings in Silver Street got underway and in 1989 plans were announced for one of the north east's biggest housing refurbishment projects—involving a £2.5-million partnership—at The Clarences Estate. The 1990s brought further capital investment with the announcement that Stockton had been accepted as a City Challenge winner, with the prospect of attracting investment of £120 million over the next five years—including considerable government funding. Under this programme there was to be neighbourhood regeneration at Blue Hall, Queens Park and Portrack and Tilery, as well as the updating of the Eastern Industrial Estates, and revitalisation of the town centre.

Chapter Twenty

Suburban Growth and Outlying Settlements

Until the early 20th century there was little housing or industrial development west of the North Eastern Railway line. Higher quality housing had been constructed on Oxbridge estate, the adjacent Wells Villas, and on the Fairfield Building estate—while the opening of the tramway between Norton and Stockton on 16 July 1898 resulted in the development of housing adjacent to Norton Road.

Settlements at East Hartburn and Preston—originally small agricultural communities—were enlarged at the end of the 19th century by construction of residences for local businessmen and industrialists (including the Head family at Hartburn Hall and the Raimes family at Hartburn Lodge). Sectors of land closer to the town centre were developed with housing at around the turn of the century—the property at the junction of Durham Road and Bishopton Road displays the detail 'Newtown Corner 1897' and the red-brick terrace on Hartburn Lane (close to the junction with Yarm Lane) has the date '1902' on the upper level. Contemporary maps often showed claypits in close proximity to the housing and it seems that clay for bricks was excavated close to the construction site.

The inter-war years brought housing expansion on the town's northern and western perimeters with schemes which included Grays (Grange) in 1920, Blue Hall in 1922 and Grangefield in 1927, followed by Eastbourne and New Blue Hall in the mid 1930s.

During the post-war years there has been considerable expansion of housing estates at Fairfield (from 1948), Roseworth (1949), Portrack (1954) and Hardwick (from 1957). Sectors close to the town centre at Tilery and Parkfield were redeveloped in 1967 and 1971 respectively, while a major building programme got underway at Elm Tree Farm from 1976.

For centuries Stockton has been a major business and trading centre for much of south-east Durham and small settlements to the west and north have strong traditional links with the town.

128 Hardwick Hall, situated close to Harrowgate Lane. Built in the late 1870s, it was owned for some years by I.C.I. Ltd. and occupied by Lord Fleck.

129 Hardwick Hall. Unoccupied for several years in the post-war period, it was demolished in the late 1980s to make way for housing.

130   St John's church, Elton. The building was extensively restored in 1841 but retains some Norman masonry and a fine chancel arch.

131   Elton House, the former rectory.

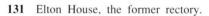

Elton, Long Newton, and Sadberge are situated alongside the west-bound route from Stockton to Darlington and in the 18th century a section of this highway was turnpiked. Elton is an example of a shrunken village with the earlier medieval settlement spreading to the south and west of the present site. Excavations by Cleveland County Archaeology Department in the last months of 1991 and 1993 uncovered part of a medieval farmstead close to Town End Farm and provided information about farming methods and living conditions during the 14th century.

Elton church was restored in 1841 but retains its original round-arched Norman doorway and Norman chancel arch with beakhead decoration. The impressive rood screen was designed by J. N. Cooper in 1907 and a stone figure on the north side of the church is probably Robert Gower who lived at nearby Coatham Stob (and died there in 1315). Elton Hall dates from the early 1900s and replaced an earlier building adjacent to the roadside. It was re-styled in 1914 by Stanley Appleby and was then the residence of Colonel Sutton. After the Second World War—when it was occupied by army personnel—the hall was used as business premises and is now a private nursing home. The white bungalow on nearby land was the gardener's cottage and Elton House was originally the rectory.

Long Newton has seen considerable growth since 1969 and several of the early features have disappeared to make way for modern housing. St Mary's church dates from 1857 and is of the Gothic revival design. Connections with the Londonderry family are to be found throughout the village and the north side of the chancel is dominated by the Vane Mausoleum (a memorial to Sir Henry Vane Tempest) and family vaults are situated beneath the east end of the church. The adjacent vicarage dates from the 16th century and is now privately owned.

The Wilson Institute was provided by a former rector in 1887 for educational purposes and is still in use for community meetings and sporting activities. Directly opposite is the perimeter wall of the old manor house.

The *Londonderry Arms* is the third building to occupy the site. Premises erected for the use of Lord Londonderry replaced the first property—'The Grey Horse'—but these became derelict and were pulled down in the early

132 Properties in the centre of Elton village.

133 Elton Hall. Built in the early 1900s, it was for some years the home of the Sutton family and after use by business companies it is now a retirement home.

1960s. Existing buildings were constructed during 1962 and the earlier outbuildings and stables were retained alongside.

There are records of a school in Long Newton during 1866 and six years later the rector, the Rev. Jonathan Wilson, organised an appeal for a new building. These premises continued in use until 1966 and they have now been adapted as a community centre. Until 1974 primary age children travelled to Sadberge but new premises were officially opened in the village on 5 March 1974.

Housing was completed at the south east end of the village around Christmas 1949 (Grasscroft) and in 1956 (Castlereagh Close). Further housing development along the northern perimeter of the village has continued during the last 20 years.

Sadberge is situated on high ground astride an important north-south Roman highway (Ryknield Street) and during the medieval period it assumed considerable administrative importance. The Wapentake of Sadberge stretched from the coast to Middleton in

Teesdale (including Stockton) and was bought by Bishop Pudsey of Durham from King Richard I in 1189.

St Andrew's church was built in 1830 in the Early English style and replaced a Norman church (dating from 1266). There are suggestions that a Roman camp and medieval castle were sited on the land close to the church but so far no documentary or material evidence has been discovered in support of these claims.

A boulder at the centre of the village green—unearthed when the nearby reservoir was under construction—celebrates Queen Victoria's golden jubilee in 1887 and highlights her title—'Countess of Sadberge'. The *Buck Inn* celebrates the name of a well-known local family during the 16th century and the *Three Tunns* housed the Assize Court until the early 19th century.

The former red-brick school building is now the village institute and new premises at the east end of the settlement provide primary education for local children. Recent housing development has expanded the size of the village and it retains a vibrancy and community spirit

134 St Mary's church, Long Newton.

135 Former smithy in the centre of Long Newton. It was latterly in use as a garage before demolition in the late 1980s to make way for housing.

136 *(Above)* Wilson Institute, Long Newton. The building was erected in 1887 for recreational and community use. Building costs were met by the village's rector.

137 *(Left)* Wesleyan church, Long Newton, with a fine red brick and terracotta frontage. It was demolished in the early 1990s to make way for housing.

138 Cottages at Sadberge. One has the date 1748 above the doorway.

139 Sadberge Methodist chapel stands alongside the line of the Roman road which ran northwards to the frontier bases.

which were probably its hallmark during the medieval period.

Redmarshall has expanded with modern housing beyond the heart of the tiny agricultural community. It is dominated by the fine church dedicated to St Cuthbert which includes Norman work in the tower and in the nave walls and chancel arch. A chapel was added in about A.D. 1300 and it now contains effigies of Thomas de Langton and his wife (dating from about 1440). The circular font is fashioned from Frosterly marble and, along with the distinctive pews, it gives the building a distinctive atmosphere.

The adjacent village of Carlton is said to be a good example of a planned medieval village with parallel rows of houses facing each other across a long, narrow green. Gardens at the rear of properties spread to the boundaries of medieval open fields surrounding the village, leaving much of the probable 11th-century layout virtually unaltered.

Thorpe Thewles stands on the original route from Stockton to Durham city. It was developed as an estate village of nearby Wynyard Park and has also been extended in recent years by housing development. The small stone church of St James was completed in 1886-7 to replace Holy Trinity church which was in use from 1849-86. At the centre of the village, the brick-built *Vane Arms* probably dates from the late 17th or early 18th centuries.

Index